THE HUTTERITE COMMUNITY COOKBOOK

Dear Terry and Margo,
   We hope this will enhance your reslarch. We appreciate your friendship so very much!
      Jim & Cheri Dudley

THE HUTTERITE COMMUNITY COOKBOOK

Joanita Kant

Good Books®
Intercourse, Pennsylvania 17534

Acknowledgements and Credits

Many thanks to the photographers who contributed their work to this project: Victor Peters—cover, 13, 19; Bernd Längin—1, 5, 8, 10, 11, 12b, 12c, 14, 17a, 17b, 18a, 18b, 89, 90, 157, 158, 192; Annie Griffiths Belt—2, 12a, 15, 16, 20, 53, 55, 124, 191; Joyce Brown—6, 7, 54, 56, 123; Dawn J. Ranck—9.

Several of the handwritten recipes first appeared in *The Hutterite Cookbook,* edited by Joanita Kant and illustrated by Mary Elmore Wipf. Published by Sioux River Press, copyright © 1984 by Joanita Kant and Mary Elmore Wipf.

Design by Dawn J. Ranck
Recipes handwritten by Rosanna Ranck

THE HUTTERITE COMMUNITY COOKBOOK

Copyright © 1990 by Good Books, Intercourse, Pennsylvania 17534
International Standard Book Number: 0-934672-56-3
Library of Congress Catalog Card Number: 90-84802

Library of Congress Cataloging-in-Publication Data

Kant, Joanita.
    The Hutterite community cookbook/Joanita Kant.
        p. cm.
    Includes bibliographical references and index.
    ISBN 0-934672-56-3 (pbk.) : $12.95
    1. Cookery, Hutterite. 2. Cookery—South Dakota. I. Title.
TX715.K183   1990
641.59783—dc20

                                                                        90-84802
                                                                        CIP

Table of Contents

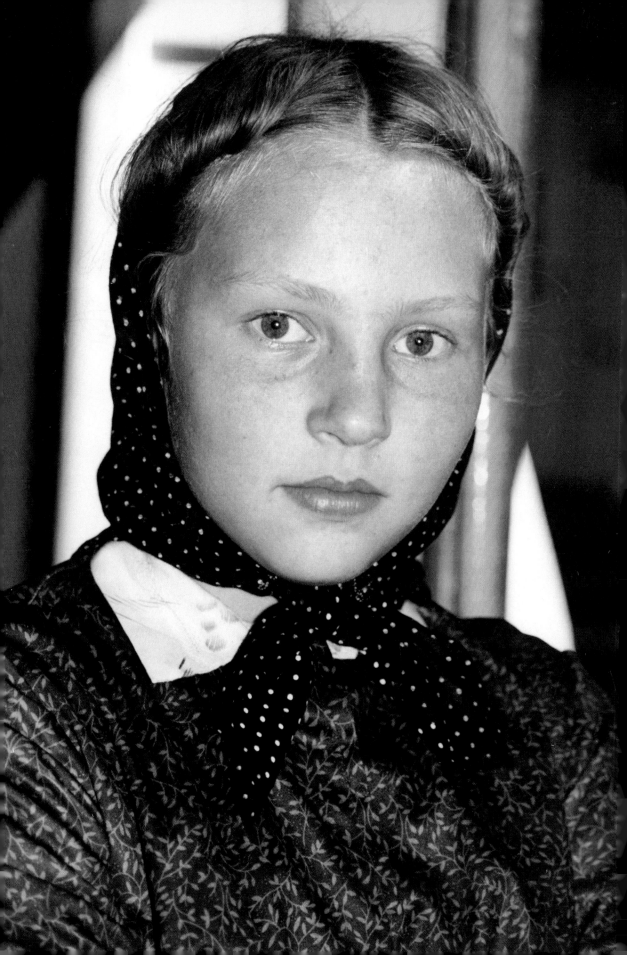

Introducing the Hutterites

A traveler roaming the vast expanses of the northern Great Plains might occasionally come upon curious, isolated clusters of neatly arranged buildings. These groupings appear to be small villages, but no public roads pass through them. The most unusual feature of these gathered buildings are long motel-like structures divided into individual family units. At each of these little settlements is a large building containing a kitchen and dining hall, and there is also a school and various kinds of barns, sheds and shops. The women wear simple, long skirts and their plainly arranged hair is covered with black head scarves patterned with white polka dots. Both men and boys wear suspenders; the men are bearded. The community speaks an Austrian dialect as well as English, but with a pronounced German accent. These people are the Hutterian Brethren or Hutterites.

History

Like the more widely known Amish and Mennonites, the Hutterites trace their origin to the sixteenth century Anabaptist movement which began in Zurich, Switzerland in 1525.

Anabaptists (rebaptizers) insisted that the true church consisted only of devout believers who were voluntarily baptized as adults. This doctrine was considered extremely radical and the Anabaptists met with severe persecution. While Anabaptism was taking root in Switzerland,

Children and adults alike live within the strong embrace of community in the huddled buildings of a Hutterite colony.

Hutterite colonies produce most of their own food and clothing. This colony also makes brooms.

other Anabaptist groups were emerging elsewhere in Europe—to the north, east and west. Within a short time Anabaptism also reached Austria, and from there Moravia (now part of Czechoslovakia) where an unusual degree of toleration was found.

In 1528 one group of Anabaptists in Moravia adopted the practice of sharing all economic goods. Although this "community of goods" developed when the group faced pressure to flee for their lives, the practice continued and eventually became one of the group's distinguishing features. Jakob Hutter was an early leader of this community, and the group was eventually nicknamed "Hutterites."

The Hutterites in Moravia grew rapidly during the sixteenth century, but in the next century war, plague and persecution greatly reduced their numbers. In 1622 Catholic rulers banished all Hutterites from Moravia. Many found refuge for a time across the border in Slovakia (also part of present Czechoslovakia, but then part of Hungary). Here, too, great pressure was put on the Hutterites to convert to Catholicism. One small group was forcibly removed to Transylvania (now central Romania).

The Hutterites in Romania were revitalized in 1755 by a group of exiled Lutherans from the Austrian province of Carinthia. The Lutherans were inspired by the teachings of the few remaining Hutterites and eventually joined them. These zealous new members insisted on following the original teachings of the group, including communal living, which had been given up about 1690.

In 1770 the Hutterites in Romania were invited to settle in the Russian Ukraine. A few Hutterites who had been forced to become Catholic in Slovakia were able to break free and join their brethren in Russia. In their new home the Hutterites experienced more freedom than they had known for over a hundred years, but, despite this freedom, they gave up their distinguishing principle of community of goods in 1819.

In 1874 virtually all the Hutterites in Russia moved to America when the Russian government threatened to take away their exemption from military service and their right to conduct their schools in the German language. Before this emigration, several Hutterite leaders were inspired to revive communal living once again. Michael Waldner began a communal group in 1859 at one Hutterite village. His followers became known as the Schmiedeleut (Blacksmith People), since Michael was a blacksmith. The next year Darius Walter started another communal group, the Dariusleut. A third group under the leadership of Jacob Wipf established community of goods after their arrival in South Dakota in 1877. These were called the Lehrerleut (Teacher People) because Wipf had been a teacher. The "Prairieleut" were the non-communal Hutterites. They settled on individual homesteads and eventually most of them joined various Mennonite groups.

The three communal groups, totalling about 400 people upon their arrival in America, developed slightly different customs over the years.

The Schmiedeleut, the largest of the three Hutterite groups, established their first colony at Bon Homme, Dakota Territory, now South Dakota, which is the oldest continuously occupied Hutterite colony. The majority of the recipes in this book come from a granddaughter colony of this original settlement.

During World War I the Hutterites were treated severely by the United States government. Two young men who were imprisoned because of their refusal to cooperate with the military died from mistreatment. This persecution caused the majority of Hutterites to move north to Canada.

Currently most Schmiedeleut live in Manitoba and South Dakota with a few in North Dakota and Minnesota. The Dariusleut and Lehrerleut live primarily in

Children are welcomed into families and community life.

Alberta, Saskatchewan and Montana. A few Dariusleut live in the state of Washington and in British Columbia. The Hutterite colony, Owa, formed in Japan in 1976.

A fourth group began in 1920 when Eberhard Arnold started a community in Germany. In 1930 Arnold affiliated with the Hutterites in North America. Arnold's followers were persecuted in Nazi Germany and took refuge in England for a time and then moved to Paraguay. By the 1960s all of the Arnold group, which adopted the name Society of Brothers, had relocated in the eastern United States. The "Arnoldleut" were fully accepted into the Hutterian Church in 1974 and have communities in New York, Connecticut, Pennsylvania, England and Germany.

Hutterite Beliefs

Hutterites affirm the basic tenets of Christianity and share distinctive Anabaptist doctrines with the Amish and conservative Mennonites. These beliefs include voluntary believer's baptism as opposed to infant baptism, non-swearing of oaths, non-resistance (a form of pacifism) and non-conformity to the world. What makes the Hutterites unique, both among their Anabaptist kinfolk and in the larger Christian world, is their all-encompassing belief in community of goods.

The Hutterian founders taught that living in community was the ultimate expression of Christian love. The brotherhood was seen as a big family, and, they reasoned, in a family all material things are shared. The Hutterites continue to believe that a true follower of Jesus will surrender all in submission to God's will and will even forsake all concern for personal property. Obedience to all of God's commands is imperative. Hutterites freely give their lives and labors in service to God and the community without monetary compensation. Taking possession of earthly things that God created for common use is considered part of the covetous, greedy spirit of the world.

The Hutterites point to the Biblical example of those converted to the first church at Jerusalem who "had all things

Large hog and farming operations create income for midwestern colonies.

in common'' (Acts 2:44,45) and other early Christians who sold all their possessions and laid them at the feet of the apostles (Acts 4:34,35).

Colony Life

In 1988 there were 35,000 Hutterian Brethren living in 374 colonies or ''Bruderhofs'' (places of the Brethren). All but a very few of these are located in the Great Plains area of Canada and the United States. In the Midwest and West there are usually between 70 and 150 people in each colony with an average of about seven people per family. When the population of a colony grows too large to maintain a sufficient amount of work for each member, the colony is divided and a new colony is started.

The Hutterites in the Midwest and West are engaged in large-scale agriculture. Colonies occupy tracts totalling 3,000 to 10,000 acres. Unlike their Amish cousins, the Hutterites have not put restrictions on the types of farm machinery they use. The very latest field equipment is utilized, and automated poultry and livestock operations are typical in the colonies.

Leadership

A preacher, selected by lot from a group nominated by the men of the colony and the preachers from other colonies, is the spiritual leader of each colony. Often there is also an assistant preacher who may serve as a German teacher. The steward or ''boss'' is elected by majority vote and is responsible for the financial management of the colony, as well as supervising the colony's labor force. Individual foremen are responsible for each agricultural, maintenance or manufacturing operation, such as the cattleman, hogman, poultryman, dairyman, carpenter, mechanic and blacksmith. There are also supervisors among the women, which include the head cook, the head seamstress, the gardener,

Everyone is assigned a task. While the work can be physically exhausting, community members do their chores together.

A wide variety of fruits and vegetables are grown in colony gardens, orchards and vineyards.

the kindergarten teacher and, in earlier years, the midwife. Each supervisor is elected, and no colony member may choose his or her own job. In smaller colonies one person may serve in several capacities.

An executive council or assembly makes all important decisions for the colony. It consists of from five to seven men, usually elected from those in key leadership positions, and always including the minister, the steward and the farm foreman.

Hutterites live very orderly lives, according to schedule. Everyone knows exactly what he or she is to do and when to do it. The colony bell punctuates each day, calling members to rise, to eat, to work and to celebrate.

Most colonies take a one hour rest period in the middle of the day. Most of the assigned jobs for both men and women are usually completed by 6:00 p.m. And no unnecessary work is done on Sunday. During these times people engage in such activities as reading, singing, visiting or going for long walks. Often they simply enjoy time alone with their own immediate family. In many ways the ordered structure of these intentional Hutterite communities creates more free time and more time with family than many people in the modern world experience.

Each day is ended with the community gathering for a half hour of worship. Every Sunday morning there is an hour and a half church service. In most colonies worship services are held in a wing of the same building that contains the kitchen. In some communities worship services are held in the school. All Hutterite sermons are read from hand-written manuscripts copied from originals that date from the 1600s. The chant-like Hutterite style of singing comes from the same period.

Education

The everyday language of the Hutterites is "Huttrish", similar to the German dialect spoken in the Carinthian area of Austria. Children are instructed to read, write and sing in High German, by a man elected to this position. The German school sessions are conducted before and after the "English" school and on Saturday and Sunday. Every Hutterite colony has an elementary school administered by the state or province and usually staffed by a certified non-Hutterite teacher. School attendance is from age six to 15. Higher education is deemed unnecessary for the Hutterian way of life. Between the ages of about 2½ and five, children attend kindergarten in a separate building. Here older women teach the children songs, prayers and Bible stories, as well as supervise their play and meals.

Baptism and Marriage

Persons do not become full members in the Hutterian church community until they are baptized. Young Hutterites usually request baptism when they are in their twenties. After baptism, new members are given voting privileges (men only) and more responsibility in the community. Only a small percentage of Hutterites leave the faith.

Marriage typically takes place soon after baptism and is an informal requirement for full participation in community responsibilities. Hutterite young people are free to choose their own mates. A young man usually selects a wife from outside his home colony, and the bride nearly always comes to her husband's colony to live. It is unusual for a Hutterite husband and wife not to be in some way related to each other since there are only fourteen traditional Hutterite family names. Few Hutterites remain single.

The Hutterite Food Tradition

Food preparation is serious business in a Hutterite colony. Some 85 to 100 people, hard-working adults as well as active children, come to the communal dining room for three meals each day. The food Hut-

Every colony has its own elementary school administered by the state or province.

terites eat is sturdy, much of it made from traditional recipes and a lot of it grown and produced on the colony's farmland and pastures.

While their principle of simplicity influences them to create basic and robust dishes, the Hutterites fill their tables plentifully and then enjoy what they eat. Careful planning makes that possible.

The Hutterites are people of the land, familiar with the seasons and acquainted with soil and rainfall and their effects on gardens and livestock. Consequently, they raise bountiful vegetables and hearty pork, beef and poultry. In addition, they have a high regard for their past. The foods they learned in central and eastern Europe have adapted well to North America. Hutterite menus include buns, dumplings, buckwheat sausage and homemade noodles.

The recipes for these dishes, many of which originated in Russia, are kept in handwritten notebooks which have been handed down from generation to generation. It is a tradition among the Hutterites that each time a colony divides to form a new daughter colony (usually when the population reaches about 120 people), the wife of the newly elected boss is given a copy of the cookbook from the mother colony. She is usually elected to be the head cook at the new colony, a pattern which has gone on for many eras and appears likely to continue.

Much of these people's diet reflects their central European origins. Meat is served abundantly; breads, buns and dumplings are made in a variety of forms for breakfast, lunch or supper; pickled vegetables and watermelon are favorites

Bun baking, cake decorating, cheese making—all contribute to the spirit of community as well as the nourishment of bodies.

and offset the heavier meat dishes.

Contrary to the practice of restaurant managers or supervisors of institutional food services, the head cook does not place regular orders with wholesale food suppliers. Instead she oversees the producing of the community's food within the colony itself, working in cooperation with their colony's hogman, cattleman and poultry manager, as well as the head gardener who sees that the garden is cultivated. While nearly self-sufficient food-wise, Hutterite colonies do buy flour, sugar, cake mixes, spices, margarine, coffee and tea. That traffic with the larger world has created an avenue for new recipes to enter the Hutterite menu. Gelatin boxes, cake mix packages and candy bags all offer tempting dishes to these cooks who enjoy the certainty of traditional foods, but also like the chance to experiment with different ingredients and combinations. That mix of old and new recipes is reflected in this collection. **The Hutterite Community Cookbook** includes the spread of dishes currently eaten in the Sunset Colony in Britton, South Dakota, a granddaughter of the first Schmiedeleut Hutterite Colony in North America. The span is wide—from mid-nineteenth century Russian favorites to dishes built around modern convenience foods.

The whole community gathers at mealtimes, with the exception of the children who are 14 years old or younger. (House children, from birth to age 2½, eat in their family apartments. Children from 2½ to five years old take their meals in the kindergarten building. Those between the ages of five and 14 eat in the children's dining room, a separate room at one end of the communal kitchen building.) The communal kitchen, dining hall and church facilities are centrally located within the colony, usually along with the school. The centrality of these buildings is symbolic of the importance of what goes on within them. A community, based upon sharing the most basic of resources and providing counsel, support and discipline for each other, must have frequent gathered times. Meeting regularly for meals is a natural way to strengthen the bond of community, as it is in any family.

Children and young adults eat and play with their respective age groups.

The Hutterite Community Cookbook

This collection of recipes is based upon the main cookbook, as well as the canning cookbook, used today in the Sunset Colony located in eastern South Dakota. This community of Schmiedeleut Hutterites is descended from the first and largest group of Hutterites to arrive in North America. While their family genealogies and religious practices have endured, their food traditions have changed more dramatically. This is, after all, a living community and not an historical society—and the acculturating influence of canning ring boxes and Sure-Jel packages has broadened the community's menu. In addition, nutritional concerns have altered some customs—desserts are served more sparingly than they once were, and the head cook has begun reducing the amounts of butter,

sugar and salt in the cooking.

At the tops of the pages in **The Hutterite Community Cookbook** are the recipes from the hand-written head cook's cookbook as used in the colony. Below each community-sized recipe is the same recipe in reduced form for an average household's use. These versions with smaller quantities have been tested so that Hutterite food can be enjoyed outside the community.

Food, for the Hutterites, is a practical matter. When the average time they spend eating a meal is 15 minutes (and much of that in near silence), it is clear that food is regarded as a necessity and not an art form. Yet the food's highly substantial qualities, the amount of time and energy it requires in its preservation and preparation, its role at moments of community celebrations, place good eating near the center of daily life in a Hutterite colony.

Children from 2 1/2 to five years old take their meals in the kindergarten building.

COOKIES
—and—
BARS

Cherry Winks

27 cups flour
12 tsp. baking flour
3 tsp. baking soda
6 tsp. salt
9 cups margarine
    or 4½ lbs.
12 cups sugar

24 eggs
1½ cups milk
12 tsp. vanilla
12 cups chopped nuts
12 cups chopped dates
4 cups cherries
30 cups corn flakes

Heat oven to 375°. Sift together dry ingredients. Set aside. Combine margarine and sugar. Cream well. Add eggs, vanilla and milk. Mix well. Blend in dry ingredients. Add chopped dates, nuts and cherries. Mix well. Form cookie-sized balls. Roll in corn flakes and press a cherry in the middle of each. Bake as usual.

Cherry Winks

Makes about 4 dozen 2½" cookies

2¼ cups flour
1 tsp. baking powder
½ tsp. baking soda
½ tsp. salt
¾ cup margarine, softened
1 cup sugar
2 eggs

1 tsp. vanilla
⅛ cup milk
1 cup chopped dates
1 cup chopped nuts
⅓ cup chopped maraschino
    cherries
2½ cups corn flakes, crushed

1. Sift together dry ingredients and set aside.
2. Combine margarine and sugar. Cream well.
3. Add eggs, vanilla and milk. Mix well.
4. Blend in dry ingredients.
5. Add chopped dates, nuts and cherries. Mix well.
6. Form into balls, 1″ in diameter, and roll them in corn flakes.
7. Press a cherry in the middle of each and bake for 8 minutes
    at 375°.

Candy Cookies

8 cups butter
14 cups white sugar
30 cups chopped dates
30 tsp. vanilla
30 eggs, well beaten

30 Tbsp. milk
15 tsp. salt
60 cups Rice Krispies
1 gal. chopped nuts
flaked coconut, as much
as possible

Heat until sugar is dissolved in butter. Add dates. Cook slowly until mushy. Add vanilla, eggs, milk and salt. Cook for two more minutes. Remove from heat and let cool. Add nuts and Rice Krispies. Roll in balls and then roll in flaked coconut. Put on waxed paper in freezer until cooled and chilled.

Candy Cookies

Makes about 3 dozen cookies

¾ cup butter
1½ cups sugar
3 cups chopped dates
3 tsp. vanilla
3 eggs, well beaten

3 Tbsp. milk
½ tsp. salt
6 cups Rice Krispies
1½ cups chopped nuts
2 cups flaked coconut

1. Heat butter and stir in sugar until sugar is dissolved.
2. Add dates and cook until mushy.
3. Add vanilla, eggs, milk and salt.
4. Cook for 2 more minutes.
5. Remove from heat and let cool.
6. Add nuts and Rice Krispies .
7. Shape into balls and then roll in flaked coconut.
8. Put on waxed paper in freezer until chilled. (Do not bake.)

Apple Sauce Cookies

4½ lbs. butter
6 lbs. sugar
12 eggs
12 cups applesauce
6 cups raisins
23 cups flour
    or a little more

2 Tbsp. baking powder
¼ cup soda
⅛ cup salt
⅓ cup cinnamon
12 cups corn flakes
6 cups walnuts

Beat butter, sugar and eggs. Blend in applesauce and raisins. Add flour, baking powder, soda, salt and cinnamon. Add corn flakes and walnuts. Bake at 400° until nice and brown.

Applesauce Cookies

Makes about 4 dozen cookies

¾ cup butter or margarine, softened
1 cup sugar
2 eggs
2 cups applesauce
1 cup raisins
4 cups flour

1 tsp. baking powder
½ tsp. baking soda
½ tsp. salt
2 tsp. cinnamon
2 cups corn flakes
1 cup walnuts, chopped

1. Beat butter, sugar and eggs together.
2. Blend in applesauce and raisins.
3. Add flour, baking powder, soda, salt and cinnamon.
4. Add corn flakes and walnuts.
5. Bake at 350° until brown.

Coconut Oatmeal Cookies from Spink Colony

7½ cups margarine   22½ cups oatmeal
15 cups brown sugar   ¼ cup vanilla
   (3¾ qt.)   7½ tsp. salt
15 eggs   3¾ tsp. baking soda
5½ cups milk   11½ Tbsp. baking powder
15 cups shredded coconut 22½ cups flour (5½ qt.)

Cream butter. Add sugar gradually, stirring all of
the time. Add well-beaten eggs. Slowly add milk.
Add oatmeal, coconut and vanilla. Set aside. Mix
dry ingredients. Combine. Drop teaspoonsful onto
cookie sheet and bake for about 15 minutes at
375°.

Coconut Oatmeal Cookies from Spink Colony

Spink Colony is situated along the James River in Spink County,
South Dakota, north of Huron, South Dakota.

Makes about 15 dozen 2½" cookies

¾ cup butter or margarine,
  softened
1½ cups brown sugar
2 eggs, well beaten
½ cup milk
2¼ cups oatmeal

1½ cups shredded coconut
1 tsp. vanilla
½ tsp. salt
1 tsp. baking soda
1 tsp. baking powder
2¼ cups flour

1. Cream the butter and add sugar gradually.
2. Mix in the well-beaten eggs.
3. Slowly add the milk.
4. Blend in oatmeal, coconut and vanilla. Set aside.
5. Mix dry ingredients, then combine with above.
6. Drop by teaspoonsful onto greased cookie sheet.
7. Bake for about 8 minutes at 350°.

Banana Cookies

10 cups shortening
 or 5 lbs.
13½ cups brown sugar,
 firmly packed
14 eggs, beaten
4½ Tbsp. vanilla
26½ cups sifted flour

4½ Tbsp. baking powder
3½ tsp. salt
3½ Tbsp. baking soda
2½ cups milk
6¾ cups chopped walnuts
13½ cups rolled oats
12½ cups mashed bananas,
 drained

Beat shortening. Add sugar and beat well. Add eggs. Set aside. Sift together flour, baking powder, salt and baking soda. Add to above mixture. Slowly add milk, vanilla, oatmeal, walnuts and bananas. Beat well after adding each ingredient. Bake like all cookies at 350°.

Banana Cookies

Makes about 4 dozen cookies

1 cup shortening
1⅓ cups brown sugar, firmly packed
2 eggs, beaten well
2½ cups sifted flour
½ Tbsp. baking powder
½ tsp. salt

½ Tbsp. baking soda
¼ cup milk
½ tsp. vanilla
1⅓ cups rolled oats
⅔ cup chopped walnuts
1⅛ cups mashed bananas, drained

1. Beat shortening and add sugar. Beat well.
2. Add eggs and set aside.
3. Sift together flour, baking powder, salt and soda. Add to the above mixture.
4. Slowly add milk, vanilla, rolled oats, walnuts and bananas. Beat well after adding each ingredient.
5. Drop by teaspoonsful onto greased cookie sheet and bake at 350° until golden brown.

Ice Box Ginger Snaps

12 cups shortening   12 tsp. cinnamon
24 cups white sugar   12 tsp. ginger
36 eggs, beaten   24 tsp. baking soda
7½ cups brown molasses   12 tsp. baking powder
54 cups flour   6 tsp salt

Whip sugar and shortening together. Add the beaten eggs and molasses. Set aside. Sift the dry ingredients together and blend with the above mixture. Shape into long rolls. Wrap in waxed paper and chill overnight in cooler. Slice and bake at 400° for about 8 minutes.

Ice-Box Ginger Snaps

Makes about 5 dozen cookies

2 cups sugar	1 tsp. cinnamon
1 cup shortening	1 tsp. ginger
3 eggs, beaten	2 tsp. baking soda
⅔ cup molasses	1 tsp. baking powder
4½ cups flour	½ tsp. salt

1. Whip sugar and shortening together.
2. Add beaten eggs and molasses. Set aside.
3. Sift the dry ingredients together and blend with the above mixture.
4. Shape into long rolls.
5. Wrap in waxed paper and chill well.
6. Slice and bake at 350° until golden brown.

Oatmeal Cookies

6¾ lbs. all purpose flour, 7½ tsp. baking soda
   or 5 qts.   1½ Tbsp. salt
4 lbs butter   5 lbs. oatmeal or 5 qt.
3½ lbs. sugar   ½ cup water
3½ lbs. brown sugar ½ cup vanilla
25 eggs

Sift together flour, salt and soda. Set aside. Blend butter, sugar, vanilla and water together. Beat in eggs. Add flour mixture. Mix well and stir in oatmeal. Bake at 325° for 10 to 12 minutes.

Oatmeal Cookies

Makes about 6 dozen cookies

4 cups flour
1½ tsp. baking soda
¾ tsp. salt
¾ cup butter, softened
1½ cups granulated sugar
1¾ cups brown sugar
1 tsp. vanilla
1½ Tbsp. water
5 eggs
4 cups oatmeal

1. Sift together flour, soda and salt and set aside.
2. Blend butter, sugars, vanilla and water together. Beat in eggs.
3. Add flour mixture. Mix well and stir in oatmeal.
4. Drop by teaspoonsful onto greased cookie sheet. Bake at 350° till golden brown.

Fork Cookies

6 qts. brown sugar
4½ lbs. margarine
36 eggs
8 Tbsp. baking soda

8 Tbsp. cream of tartar
12 tsp. ginger
12 tsp. vanilla
10½ qts. flour

Beat margarine and sugar together until nice. Beat in eggs. When nice and fluffy, add flour, to which soda, cream of tartar and ginger has been added. Roll into balls and press flat with fork. Bake for 8 to 10 minutes at 300°.

Fork Cookies

Makes about 5 dozen cookies

¾ cup margarine, softened
2 cups brown sugar
3 eggs
1 tsp. baking soda

1½ tsp. cream of tartar
1 tsp. ginger
3½ cups flour
1 tsp. vanilla

1. Beat margarine and sugar together. Beat in eggs.
2. Sift soda, cream of tartar, ginger and flour together. Add to wet ingredients and stir in vanilla.
3. Roll into balls and press flat with a fork.
4. Bake at 350° until golden brown.

Carrot Cookies

3¾ qt. sugar or 15 cups   15 tsp. vanilla
5¾ lbs. margarine   15 tsp. lemon
   or 11¼ cups   5 tsp. salt
9½ lbs. flour or 30 cups   15 cups ground carrots
15 tsp. baking powder   15 eggs

Blend butter, add sugar and beaten eggs. Add flour, baking powder and salt. Beat well. Add vanilla, lemon and carrots. Bake at 350° until golden brown.

Carrot Cookies

Makes about 5 dozen cookies

1½ cups butter or margarine	**½ tsp. salt**
1½ cups sugar	**2 tsp. vanilla**
2 eggs	**2 tsp. lemon flavoring**
3¾ cups flour	**1¾ cups ground carrots**
1½ tsp. baking powder	

1. Whip butter, then add sugar and beaten eggs, blending well.
2. Add flour, baking powder and salt and beat well.
3. Add vanilla, lemon flavoring and carrots.
4. Drop by teaspoonsful onto greased cookie sheet and bake at 350° until golden brown.

Chocolate Drop Marshmallow Cookies

4 cups margarine
8 cups sugar
8 eggs, well beaten
14 cups flour
4 tsp. baking soda

2 tsp. salt
2 cups cocoa
4 cups milk
¼ cup vanilla
4 cups chopped walnuts and marshmallows

Mix sugar, margarine, eggs and vanilla until creamy. Sift together flour, baking soda, salt and cocoa. Blend into creamy mixture, alternately with milk. Stir in walnuts and drop by teaspoonful onto greased cookie sheet. Bake for 8 minutes. Remove from oven and press marshmallows lightly into cookie. Return to the oven and bake for two more minutes or until cookies are done and marshmallows are softened. Oven should be 325°.

Chocolate Drop Marshmallow Cookies

Makes 3 dozen cookies

1 cup sugar
½ cup margarine, softened
1 egg, well beaten
1 tsp. vanilla
1¾ cups flour
½ tsp. baking soda

¼ tsp. salt
¼ cup cocoa
½ cup milk
½ cup chopped walnuts
3 dozen regular size
  marshmallows

1. Mix sugar, margarine, egg and vanilla until creamy.
2. Sift together flour, baking soda, salt and cocoa. Blend this into the creamy mixture, alternately with milk.
3. Stir in walnuts and drop batter by teaspoonful onto greased cookie sheet.
4. Bake for 8 minutes at 325°; then remove from oven and press a marshmallow lightly into each cookie.
5. Return to oven and bake for 2 more minutes until marshmallows are softened.

White Cookies

6 lbs. flour
6 lbs. cake flour
1 cup baking powder
4 tsp. salt
3¾ lbs. butter

7½ lbs. sugar
30 eggs
11⅛ cups milk
4½ cups walnuts

Cream butter and sugar together. Beat until creamy. Add eggs. Set aside. Sift flour, salt and baking powder together. Add to above mixture, with milk. Beat well after each addition. For chocolate cookies, take half of the dough and add 1¼ cups Hershey's cocoa. Bake at 325° for about 8 to 10 minutes.

White Cookies

Makes about 5 dozen cookies

1 cup butter, softened
1 cup sugar
3 eggs
1½ cups all-purpose flour
1½ cups cake flour

½ tsp. salt
2 tsp. baking powder
1½ cups milk
½ cup walnuts

1. Beat butter and sugar together until creamy.
2. Add eggs. Set aside.
3. Sift flours, salt and baking powder together. Add to creamy mixture along with milk, beating well after each addition. Stir in walnuts.
4. Drop by teaspoonsful onto greased cookie sheet. Bake until golden brown at 350°.

Variation: To make half the batch chocolate cookies, add ½ cup sweetened cocoa powder to half the dough before baking.

Rice Krispies Cookies

6 lbs. butter
5½ lbs. white sugar
4¾ lbs brown sugar
24 eggs
2 Tbsp. salt
¼ cup baking powder
¼ cup baking soda

½ cup vanilla
8 lbs. flour
1½ qts. coconut
1½ qts. corn flakes
1½ boxes of Rice Krispies
3 lbs. oatmeal

Cream together butter, sugar, eggs and salt. Blend well. Add dry ingredients which have been sifted together. Add oatmeal, coconut, Rice Krispies and corn flakes. Drop by spoonfuls onto cookie sheet and bake for 8 to 10 minutes at 375°.

Rice Krispies Cookies

Makes 4 dozen cookies

1 cup butter, softened
1 cup granulated sugar
¾ cup brown sugar
2 eggs
½ tsp. salt
1 tsp. baking powder
1 scant tsp. baking soda

1½ cups flour
1 tsp. vanilla
1 cup oatmeal
½ cup coconut
1 cup Rice Krispies
1 cup corn flakes

1. Cream together butter, sugars and eggs, blending well.
2. Sift together salt, baking powder, baking soda and flour. Stir into creamy ingredients. Blend in vanilla.
3. Add oatmeal, coconut, Rice Krispies and corn flakes.
4. Drop by teaspoonsful onto cookie sheet and bake at 350° until golden brown.

Cookie Fudge - Cooked

6 cups syrup

6 cups sugar

6 cups thin cream

5 packages Rice Krispies

2½ boxes corn flakes

5 cups coconut

5 cups nuts

Cook together syrup, sugar and cream until it forms a soft ball when dropped in cold water. Pour this over a mixture of the Rice Krispies, corn flakes, coconut and nuts. Press into large buttered pan. Cool and cut into square pieces.

Cookie Fudge

Makes 9" x 13" pan of bars

½ cup corn syrup

½ cup sugar

½ cup thin cream

2 cups corn flakes

4 cups Rice Krispies

½ cup coconut

½ cup nuts

1. Cook together syrup, sugar and cream until it forms a soft ball when dropped in cold water. Boil slowly.
2. Pour this over a mixture of corn flakes, Rice Krispies, coconut and nuts.
3. Press into a 9" x 13" buttered pan.
4. Cool and cut into square pieces.

Chocolate Chip Cookies for Sunset Colony

8 cups butter (4 lbs.)   30 cups flour, approximately
9 cups brown sugar   12 tsp. soda
9 cups white sugar   12 tsp. salt
12 tsp. vanilla   4 cups nuts
2 cups water   12 packages of 12 oz. chocolate
24 eggs   chips or 24 cups

Beat butter and sugar together. Add beaten eggs, vanilla and water. Sift the dry ingredients together and add to the above mixture. Blend well. Add nuts and chocolate chips. Drop by teaspoonful onto cookie sheet and bake till golden brown. Bake at 350° for about 8 to 10 minutes.

Chocolate Chip Cookies for Sunset Colony

Makes about 3 dozen cookies

¾ cup butter or margarine, softened
¾ cup brown sugar
¾ cup white sugar
3 eggs, beaten
1 tsp. vanilla

3 tsp. water
2½ cups flour
1 tsp. baking soda
½ tsp. salt
½ cup nuts, chopped
1 pkg. (12 oz.) chocolate chips

1. Beat butter and sugars together. Add beaten eggs, vanilla and water.
2. Sift the dry ingredients together and add to the above mixture. Blend well.
3. Add nuts and chocolate chips.
4. Drop by teaspoonful onto greased cookie sheet. Bake at 350° for about 8 minutes.

Dream Bars

9 cups butter	18 tsp. vanilla
7⅜ qts. brown sugar	4½ tsp. salt
19 cups sifted flour	9 tsp. baking powder
2½ cups cocoa	9 cups chopped nuts
36 eggs, beaten	18 cups shredded coconut

Blend together butter, 4½ cups sugar and 15 cups flour. Press in bottom of pan and bake at 300° for 10 minutes. Combine eggs, vanilla, remaining sugar and salt. Mix thoroughly. Set aside. Sift together remaining flour, baking powder and cocoa. Add to egg mixture and beat. Add nuts and coconut. Remove pans from oven and pour this mixture on top. Return to oven and bake 30 to 40 minutes longer. This makes 12 pans.

Dream Bars

Makes a 9" x 13" pan of 15–18 bars

½ cup butter, softened	½ tsp. salt
1½ cups brown sugar	½ tsp. baking powder
1 cup flour	⅛ cup cocoa powder
2 eggs, beaten	1 cup shredded coconut
1 tsp. vanilla	½ cup nuts

1. Blend together butter, ¼ cup of the sugar and ¾ cup of the flour.
2. Press in bottom of pan and bake at 300° for 10 minutes.
3. Combine eggs, vanilla, remaining sugar and salt.
4. Mix thoroughly. Set aside.
5. Sift together remaining flour, baking powder and cocoa.
6. Add to egg mixture and beat.
7. Add coconut and nuts.
8. Remove crust from oven and pour the mixture over the crust.
9. Return to oven and bake 30 to 40 minutes longer.

Fig Filled Cookies

(handwritten card)

Fig Filled Cookies

15¾ cups brown sugar
15¾ cups white sugar
8¼ lbs. margarine
32 eggs

3⅛ Tbsp. salt
16¼ qts. flour
10½ Tbsp. baking powder
10½ Tbsp. vanilla

Cream together butter, sugar and eggs. Beat thoroughly. Add sifted dry ingredients, then vanilla. Pat dough ½ inch thick. Spread with cooked filling. Cover with same size dough. Cut up into 2 or 3 inch squares. Bake at 325° for 10 minutes or until golden brown.

Fig Filling

2 cups sugar
2½ tsp. vanilla
6 lbs. figs

¾ qt. raisins
5 cups water
3 cups dried apples

Grind figs, raisins and apples using attachment with largest holes. Then cook until nice and mushy or until all of the water is mixed up.

Fig Filled Cookies

Makes about 4 dozen cookies

¾ cup butter or margarine, softened
1 cup brown sugar
1 cup white sugar
3 eggs, beaten

½ tsp. salt
1 Tbsp. baking powder
3½ cups flour
1 tsp. vanilla

1. Cream together butter, sugars and eggs. Beat them thoroughly.
2. Add sifted dry ingredients, then the vanilla.
3. Pat half of dough into rectangle ½″ thick.
4. Spread with cooked filling (see page 40).
5. Cover with same size rectangle of dough.
6. Cut into 2″ or 3″ squares and place on a greased cookie sheet.
7. Bake at 350° till golden brown.

Date Filled Cookies

9 cups butter
27 cups flour
27 cups oatmeal
18 cups brown sugar

8 cups milk
18 tsp. baking soda
36 tsp. baking powder

Cream together butter, brown sugar. Add milk. Add dry ingredients. Like piecrust, roll dough thin on lightly floured board. Cut with round cookie cutter. Place a teaspoon of cooked filling in center of each and cover with identical piece of dough. Seal edges. Bake in moderate oven at 350° until golden brown.

Date Filling

2 cups sugar
2½ tsp. vanilla
8 lbs. dates

8 cups water
4 cups dried apples

Cook in saucepan until mushy. Stir often. Set aside.

Date Filled Cookies

Makes about 4 dozen cookies

1 cup butter, softened
2 cups brown sugar
¾ cup milk
3 cups flour

3 cups oatmeal
¾ tsp. baking soda
2 tsp. baking powder

1. Cream together butter and brown sugar.
2. Add milk.
3. Add dry ingredients.
4. Roll out dough as thin as a pie crust on a lightly floured board. Cut with round cookie cutter.
5. Place a teaspoon of cookie filling (see page 40) in the center of each circle and cover with an identical piece of dough. Seal edges.
6. Bake at 350° until golden brown.

Pinwheel Refrigerator Date Cookies

7 cups brown sugar   3 tsp. salt
7 cups granulated sugar   28 cups sifted flour
7 cups butter   14 tsp. baking powder
14 eggs   14 tsp. vanilla

Cream together butter, sugar and eggs. Beat thoroughly. Add sifted dry ingredients. Add vanilla. Pat dough ½ inch thick. Prepare filling.

Filling

6 lbs dates and   5 cups water
4 cups figs   6 tsp. vanilla
5 cups sugar

Blend filling ingredients and cook, stirring constantly until thick. Cool. Add vanilla. Spread on dough. Roll up like a jelly roll. Wrap in waxed paper. Chill overnight in refrigerator. Cut into slices to form cookies. Bake at 375°.

Pinwheel Refrigerator Date Cookies

Makes about 4 dozen cookies

1 cup butter or margarine, softened	½ tsp. salt
1 cup brown sugar	4 cups flour
1 cup granulated sugar	2 tsp. baking powder
2 eggs	2 tsp. vanilla

1. Cream together butter, sugars and eggs. Beat thoroughly.
2. Add sifted, dry ingredients and vanilla. Pat or roll out dough to ½" thickness.
3. Prepare filling (see page 40), spread on dough and roll up like a jelly roll.
4. Wrap in waxed paper. Chill overnight in refrigerator.
5. Cut into slices to form cookies. Bake at 375°.

Fig Filling

3 cups figs (or dates)   ⅓ cup sugar
⅓ cup raisins   1 tsp. vanilla
3 cups dried apples   ½ cup water

1. Chop figs, raisins and apples.
2. Stir together, along with sugar, vanilla and water.
3. Cook till mushy or until all the water is boiled away. Let cool.

Date Filling

½ cup sugar   ½ cup water
⅔ tsp. vanilla   1 raw, peeled, chopped apple
½ lb. chopped pitted dates
   (1 box)

1. Cook filling in saucepan until mushy, stirring often.
2. Set aside to cool.

Filling for Pinwheel Refrigerator Date Cookies

¼ cup dates   1 cup water
1 cup figs   1 tsp. vanilla
1 cup sugar

1. Chop the dates and the figs and add sugar and water.
2. Cook, stirring constantly, until thickened.
3. Cool. Add vanilla.

BREADS

Buns for Children and Women

8 qts. milk
2 qts. water
4 lbs. butter
5 cups sugar

12 eggs
½ cup salt
1 cup dry yeast
36 lbs. flour

Dissolve yeast in warm water. Add sugar and let it set for a little while. Add salt and flour last. Let dough rise for ¾ hour. Knead down. Let rise ½ hour. When full, cut up and let lie for 15 minutes. Roll 6 or 7 pans and over half an hour, make the rest of the dough. Let rise for 1 hour and 15 minutes. Bake for 1 hour at 225° before rolling second batch.

Buns for Women and Children

In some Hutterite colonies the women eat together on one side of the dining room, the men sit on the opposite side. In other colonies, the men eat first, followed by the women. Children are in a separate room off the dining room.

Makes about 3 dozen buns

1 yeast cake	¼ lb. butter, softened
½ cup warm water	1 egg
¼ cup sugar	½ tsp. salt
2 cups milk	4½ cups flour

1. Dissolve yeast in warm water.
2. Add sugar and let mixture sit for several minutes. Add milk.
3. Beat butter and egg and add to yeast mixture.
4. Stir in salt and flour last.
5. Let dough rise for ¾ hour. Knead dough. Cover with cloth and let rise for 1 hour and 15 minutes.
6. When dough doubles in size, form into small buns and let rise for another 1 hour and 15 minutes in a greased pan. Bake at 375° for 15–20 minutes.

Buns for Wieners

2¼ qts. milk
¾ qt. water
¼ cup yeast
2 cups sugar
¼ cup honey

1 Tbsp. salt
¾ lb. margarine
2 eggs
10 lbs. flour or 6 ¾ qts.

Dissolve yeast in warm water. Add sugar. Let set for a few minutes. Add milk, honey, salt, margarine and eggs. Add flour last. Let rise and bake as usual, after forming into wiener bun shapes.

Buns for Wieners

Makes about 2½ dozen buns

1 yeast cake
½ cup warm water
¼ cup sugar
1 cup milk
1 tsp. honey

½ tsp. salt
1 Tbsp. margarine, softened
1 egg
3½ cups flour

1. Dissolve yeast in warm water.
2. Add sugar. Let stand for a few minutes.
3. Add milk, honey, salt, margarine and egg.
4. Add flour last.
5. Cover with cloth and let rise for 1 hour at room temperature.
6. Form into wiener-shaped buns and allow to rise another hour.
7. Bake at 375° for 15–20 minutes.

Small Bun Recipe for Wieners

3 qts. milk
1 qt. water
⅓ cup dry yeast
2 cups sugar
1 cup honey

1 lb. margarine
¼ cup salt
14 to 16 lbs. flour
or 8 full quarts
3 eggs

Dissolve yeast in warm water. Add milk, sugar and honey. Let rest. Add margarine and salt. When margarine is melted, add eggs and flour. Let rise and bake as usual.

Small Buns for Wieners

Makes about 3 dozen buns

1 yeast cake
½ cup warm water
1½ cups milk
⅛ cup sugar
1 Tbsp. honey

4 Tbsp. margarine, softened
1 tsp. salt
1 egg
4 cups flour

1. Dissolve yeast in warm water.
2. Add milk, sugar and honey. Let rest.
3. Add margarine and salt. When margarine is fully blended, add egg and flour. Let rise for 1 hour.
4. Form into small wiener-shaped buns and let rise for another hour in a greased pan.
5. Bake at 375° for 15–20 minutes.

Banana Bread

1¼ cups butter   1 tsp. salt
5 eggs   2½ cups nuts
2½ tsp. soda   5 ripe bananas
2½ cups sugar   ⅛ cup vanilla
5 cups flour

Cream butter and sugar together. Add beaten eggs
and bananas which have been mashed. Add flour,
soda and salt which have been sifted together. Add
nuts last. Bake at 350° for about 25 to 30 minutes.
This makes 3 small loaves.

Banana Bread

Makes one loaf

¼ cup butter, softened   ½ tsp. baking soda
½ cup sugar   ½ tsp. salt
1 egg, beaten   1 tsp. vanilla
1 ripe banana, mashed   ½ cup nuts
1 cup flour

1. Cream butter and sugar together.
2. Add beaten egg and mashed banana.
3. Sift together the flour, soda and salt. Blend into batter.
   Stir in vanilla.
4. Mix in nuts.
5. Bake at 350° for about 25–30 minutes.

Cinnamon Rolls

2 lbs. margarine
2 lbs. sugar
1 qt. eggs
½ qt. water, warm with ½ cup yeast, dissolved
12 lbs. flour or a little more
cinnamon, sugar and margarine to sprinkle on
prepared dough

Smooth the margarine and put in part of the sugar, along with the eggs. Make a soft dough with milk and flour. Add yeast-water mixture and the rest of the ingredients, mix well. Let dough rise for one hour. Make rolls and let rise for ¾ hour. The rolls are made as follows. Flour a table and roll out dough ¼ inch thick. Spread dough with margarine and sprinkle with cinnamon and sugar. Roll up dough and cut rolls 1 inch thick. Put 24 in a pan. Bake at 400° until nice and golden brown. Prepare icing.

Cinnamon Rolls

Makes about 4 dozen rolls

½ cup margarine, softened
½ cup sugar
½ cup eggs
1 yeast cake
¼ cup warm water

6 cups flour or a little more
cinnamon, sugar and
margarine to sprinkle on
prepared dough

1. Beat the margarine, gradually mixing in the sugar and eggs.
2. Make a soft dough with milk and flour.
3. Dissolve yeast in warm water. Add to the rest of the ingredients. Mix well.
4. Let dough rise one hour.
5. To shape into rolls, flour the table and roll out dough ¼″ thick. Spread dough with margarine and sprinkle with cinnamon and sugar. Roll up dough and cut rolls 1″ thick. Put about 12–15 in a pan. Let rise 45 minutes.
6. Bake at 400° until golden brown.
7. After rolls cool, spread with icing.

Icing for Cinnamon Rolls

4 cups egg whites and 1 tsp. salt
8 cups white syrup
3/4 cup vanilla
18 cups powdered sugar

Mix all ingredients together. Spread icing on rolls

Icing for Cinnamon Rolls

1 egg white
½ cup white corn syrup

1 tsp. vanilla
2 cups powdered sugar

Mix all ingredients together. Spread icing on rolls.

Sweet Raised Doughnuts

¼ cup dry yeast
2¾ qts. scalded and
   cooled milk
9 cups flour
9 lbs. flour or 7 qts.
1½ Tbsp. nutmeg

1½ Tbsp salt
3 cups sugar
3 cups butter
¼ cup vanilla
15 eggs

Dissolve yeast in scalded and cooled milk. Add 9 cups flour. Set aside. Cream together sugar, butter, vanilla and eggs. Add yeast mixture. Add 9 lbs. flour. Roll on floured board and cut with doughnut cutter. Let rise until double and fry as usual.

Sweet Raised Doughnuts

Makes 2½ dozen doughnuts

1 yeast cake
3¾ cups milk, scalded and
   cooled
1 cup flour
1 cup sugar
1 cup butter or margarine,
   softened

1 tsp. vanilla
5 eggs
9⅓ cups flour
½ tsp. nutmeg
½ tsp. salt

1. Dissolve yeast in scalded and cooled milk.
2. Add 1 cup flour to the yeast mixture. Set aside.
3. Cream together sugar, butter, vanilla and eggs. Stir in yeast mixture.
4. Add 9⅓ cups flour, nutmeg and salt.
5. Roll dough to ¾″ thickness on floured board and cut with doughnut cutter.
6. Let rise until double and fry in 3–4″ of fat at 375°. Turn doughnuts as they rise until golden brown.

Coating for Doughnuts

2 cups milk
½ cup margarine
2 Tbsp. vanilla
4½ qts. powdered sugar

Glaze for Doughnuts

¼ cup milk
2 Tbsp. margarine, softened
1 tsp. vanilla

2¼ cups powdered sugar, sifted

Mix together and spread on finished doughnuts.

Plain Raised Doughnuts

⅓ cup dry yeast
1½ cups warm water
1 lb. margarine
1 cup sugar

20 eggs
3 qts. milk (scalded and cooled)
3 tsp. salt
7½ to 9 qts. flour

Add yeast to warm water and dissolve completely. Cream together margarine, sugar and eggs. Add milk and yeast mixture. Add flour and salt. Roll out on floured board and cut with doughnut cutter. Let rise and fry as usual.

Plain Raised Doughnuts

Makes about 2 dozen doughnuts

1 yeast cake	**1 cup and 3 Tbsp. milk,**
2 Tbsp. warm water	**scalded and cooled**
2 Tbsp. margarine, softened	**4 cups flour**
⅛ cup sugar	**½ tsp. salt**
2 eggs	

1. Add yeast to warm water and dissolve completely.
2. Cream together margarine, sugar and eggs. Add milk and yeast mixture. Stir in flour and salt.
3. Roll out on floured board and cut with doughnut cutter. (Use as little additional flour as possible. The dough will be sticky.)
4. Allow to rise before frying in 3–4″ of fat at 375°. Remove from kettle when doughnuts are brown on both sides.

Cream Puffs

1½ lbs. butter
6 cups water
6 cups sifted flour
2 tsp. salt
24 eggs

Boil water in saucepan on high temperature. Add butter. When fully melted, add flour and salt all at once, stirring immediately. When dough leaves the sides of the pan clean, remove from burner and cool for about 20 minutes. Add eggs, one at a time, beating after each addition. Drop by spoonful onto cookie sheet, 2 Tbsp. to a puff. Bake in hot oven, 400° for about 40 to 50 minutes. When puffs are cool, fill with your choice of filling.

Cream Puffs

Makes about 1 dozen puffs

1 cup water	**1 cup sifted flour**
½ cup butter or margarine,	**½ tsp. salt**
softened	**4 eggs**

1. Bring water to a boil in saucepan. Add butter.
2. When butter is fully melted, add flour and salt all at once, stirring continuously.
3. When dough leaves the sides of the pan clean, remove from burner and cool for about 20 minutes.
4. Add eggs, one at a time, beating thoroughly after each addition.
5. Drop by spoonfuls onto greased cookie sheet, 2 Tbsp. to a puff, about 2″ apart. Bake at 400° for 35–40 minutes. When puffs are cool, fill with your choice of filling.
6. Fill with whipped cream, flavored with vanilla and sugar.

The Role of Women in Community Life

Hutterite women are active members of the community, although they do not vote nor hold positions of leadership. They are primarily caretakers with a strong loyalty to their own families and their children. They enjoy embroidering and quilting. At the daily evening church service they sing with great gusto, often drowning out the voices of the men. They visit with each other. They work hard. They complain and they rejoice. While their eyes and faces sometimes register pain and suffering, more often they reveal deep inner contentment along with a love for and an acceptance of their community and way of life.

In Hutterite life the wishes and will of the community always prevail over the rights of the individual. In fact, one of the foundational beliefs of Hutterite society is that individual members submit to and become one with the will of the community. Because of this, Hutterite women and men alike learn early in life that to survive means to enjoy working under the rules and schedules of their particular community.

Like many other plain groups (Old Order Amish, Old Order Mennonites and Old Order River Brethren, for example), Hutterites believe the Bible teaches a divine order in which God is the head, man is under God and woman is under man. Because of this understanding, Hutterite women do not participate in formal decision-making.

Men make the key decisions, but with the informal counsel of their wives. To the men falls the responsibility of leadership. They need to select colony leaders; the poultry, hog and dairy bosses; the head gardener and garden woman. In informal consultation with the female members they select the head cook, as well. The colony boss works with her to determine the amount of money available for groceries, and, in fact, he usually does the shopping. As manager of the community budget, he also works with the head tailoress to determine how many yards and what style fabric she can afford to buy. While the garden woman decides when to can, the colony boss helps to make all the necessary arrangements.

Women express their opinions privately to each other and to their husbands and fathers, but they do not vote. To many contemporary women, the lives of Hutterite women may appear oppressive and joyless. To Hutterite women, on the other hand, life without the protection and safe haven of the community is unimaginable and frightening.

Muffin Tarts

(handwritten recipe card)

Muffin Tarts

3½ lbs. margarine
2½ cups brown sugar
5 Tbsp. maple flavoring
20 eggs
3¾ qts. sifted cake flour

5 tsp. baking powder
2½ qts. raisins (less or more)
¾ qts. chopped walnuts
1½ Tbsp. salt

Cream together butter and sugar. Add maple flavoring and eggs. Beat well. Sift cake flour with salt and baking powder. Add to cream mixture. Mix well. Stir in raisins and walnuts. Bake 15 to 20 minutes at 325°. To prepare dough in muffin tins, put in one spoon of dough and one spoon of jelly, then again enough dough to make ⅔ full. You may use no jelly at all and have plain muffins if you prefer.

Muffin Tarts

Makes about 8 muffins

1 cup milk

⅓ cup butter or margarine, softened
¼ cup brown sugar
1 tsp. maple flavoring
2 eggs
1½ cups sifted cake flour

½ tsp. salt
½ tsp. baking powder
½ cup raisins
⅓ cup walnuts
jelly of your choice

1. Cream together butter and sugar.
2. Add maple flavoring and eggs. Beat thoroughly.
3. Sift cake flour with salt and baking powder. Add to creamed mixture, mixing well.
4. Stir in raisins and walnuts.
5. Place one spoon of batter in each muffin tin, top each with one spoon of jelly, then add enough batter to make each tin ⅔ full. (Plain muffins are delicious also!)
6. Bake 15–20 minutes at 350°.

Date Walnut Muffins

8 cups flour
¾ qt. sugar
15 tsp. baking powder
3 tsp. salt
6 eggs

2 cups melted butter
4½ cups milk
3 tsp. vanilla
3 cups chopped dates
3 cups chopped walnuts

Sift flour, sugar, baking powder and salt together in a medium bowl. Beat eggs slightly. Stir in, and add butter, milk and vanilla. Add all at once to the flour mixture. When evenly moist, fold in dates and nuts. Spoon into greased muffin pan cups. Fill ⅔ full. Bake for 25 minutes or until puffed and golden brown at 325°. Cool 10 minutes in pan. Remove and serve warm. Makes 72 muffins.

Date Walnut Muffins

Makes about 16 muffins

2⅔ cups flour
1 cup sugar
3 tsp. baking powder
½ tsp. salt
2 eggs
1½ cups milk

⅔ cup melted butter or
  margarine
1 tsp. vanilla
1 cup chopped dates
1 cup chopped walnuts

1. Sift flour, sugar, baking powder and salt together in a medium bowl. Set aside.
2. In a smaller bowl beat eggs slightly, then add milk, butter and vanilla.
3. Make a well in the flour mixture and pour milk mixture into it. Fold in the flour with as little stirring as possible.
4. Fold in dates and nuts.
5. Place paper muffin cups in muffin tins. Fill each ⅔ full.
6. Bake at 325° for 25 minutes or until golden brown. Cool 10 minutes in pan before removing.

Waffles for Women

2½ heaping cups flour
2 cups milk
2 cups eggs
1 cup butter
a little salt and baking powder.

Beat butter, add eggs and beat a little. add flour, milk, salt and baking powder. Fry as usual.

Waffles for Women

Makes about 1 dozen waffles

¼ cup butter
1 egg
1¼ heaping cups flour
1 cup milk

¼ tsp. salt
½ tsp. baking soda
1 tsp. baking powder

1. Cream butter. Beat in egg.
2. Stir in flour, milk, salt, baking soda and baking powder.
3. Bake on seasoned waffle iron.

Dumplings for Women

1 cup butter
1 cup eggs with 2 egg yolks included
2¾ cups sifted flour
1 Tbsp. baking powder

Cream together butter and eggs. Add flour and baking powder. Drop on broth and boil for 20 minutes. Cover and do not lift lid during cooking.

Dumplings for Women

Makes 4-6 servings

¼ cup butter, softened
1 egg
1½ cups sifted flour
1½ tsp. baking powder
1 quart meat broth

1. Cream together butter and egg.
2. Stir in flour and baking powder.
3. Drop into 1 quart boiling broth, cover and boil for 20 minutes. Do not lift lid during cooking.

These dumplings can also be steamed in a steamer for 20 minutes.

Dumplings for Sunday

6¾ lbs. butter
5 qts. eggs
10 qts. flour
2 Tbsp. baking powder

Cream together butter and eggs. Add flour and baking powder. Drop on broth and boil for 20 minutes. Cover and do not lift lid during cooking.

Dumplings for Sunday

Makes 4-6 servings

⅓ **cup butter, softened**
1 egg
2 cups flour
½ **tsp. baking powder**
1 quart meat broth

1. Cream together butter and egg.
2. Stir in flour and baking powder.
3. Drop into 1 quart boiling broth, cover and boil for 20 minutes. Do not lift lid during cooking.

These dumplings can also be steamed in a steamer for 20 minutes.

A Bread Dumpling

1½ lbs. butter
2 qts. eggs
2 medium onions

1 Tbsp. salt
6 qts. bread crumbs

Fry onion in a little fat and drain. Beat butter good and then beat in eggs. Add crumbs and onions. This is the filling for the dough.

Dough

1¼ qts. water
5 eggs
2½ qts. flour

Mix together water, eggs and flour and roll out on floured board. Fill with above mixture. Boil or steam as a regular dumpling.

A Bread Dumpling

Makes 4–6 servings

Filling

⅓ cup onions, chopped
2 Tbsp. butter
¼ cup butter, softened

3 eggs
½ tsp. salt
2 cups bread crumbs

1. Sauté onions in 2 Tbsp. butter, then drain and set aside.
2. Cream ¼ cup butter well and then beat in eggs.
3. Add salt, crumbs and onions.

Dough

⅓ cup water
1 egg

¾ cup flour

1. Mix together water, egg and flour. Roll out to ⅛" thickness on floured board.
2. Cut dough into 4" squares. Place 2 Tbsp. filling on top of each. Fold up sides of dough and seal.
3. Drop into 4" boiling water and boil for 15 minutes or steam in a steamer for 20 minutes.

Pancakes

8 cups flour
16 cups milk
35 eggs
¼ cup salt
1 cup sugar

Mix and fry as usual at 400°.

Pancakes

Makes 16 4" pancakes

2 cups flour
2 cups milk
4 eggs

½ tsp. salt
1 tsp. baking powder
2 Tbsp. sugar

1. Mix together all ingredients and stir.
2. Heat griddle until drops of water sizzle on it.
3. Use a scant ¼ cup of batter for each pancake.
4. Turn when bubbly on top.

Hot Cakes

8 qts. sour milk
2½ qts. eggs
¾ cup salt
¾ cup sugar

½ cup baking soda
1 qt. fat
6 qts. flour

Cream together sugar, eggs and fat. Add sour milk and baking soda mixed together. Sift together salt and flour. Combine all ingredients. Fry as usual.

Hot Cakes

Makes 10 4" pancakes

1 tsp. sugar
1 egg
2 Tbsp. vegetable oil
½ tsp. baking soda

1 cup sour milk (1 tsp. vinegar will sour 1 cup milk)
¼ tsp. salt
1 tsp. baking powder
1 cup flour

1. Cream together sugar, egg and oil.
2. Mix soda and milk. Stir into first mixture.
3. Sift together salt, baking powder and flour.
4. Combine all ingredients.
5. Fry hot cakes on a slightly greased griddle.

Different Pancakes

2¼ cups milk
2¼ cups flour
2¼ cups eggs
1 tsp. salt
2 slices bread

Soak bread in milk in morning until you mix other batter. Combine all ingredients. Fry as usual.

Different Pancakes

Makes 6 5" pancakes

1 slice bread	1 tsp. baking powder
1 cup milk	1 cup eggs
1 cup flour	½ tsp. salt

1. Soak bread in milk overnight.
2. Mash and blend the bread with the milk.
3. Sift baking powder with the flour.
4. Add other ingredients.
5. Fry on very hot griddle.

Potato Pancakes

5 lbs. grated potatoes   5 lbs. flour
¾ cup grated onions   ½ tsp. pepper
5 eggs, slightly beaten   salad oil for frying

Grate potatoes and onions. Drain well. Combine potatoes, onions, eggs, flour, salt and pepper. In a large skillet, heat oil ⅛ inch deep until hot but not smoking. For each pancake, drop 3 Tbsp. of dough at a time into hot fat. Flatten with spatula. Fry for 2 to 3 minutes on each side or until golden brown. Drain well on paper before serving.

Potato Pancakes

Makes about 8 pancakes

1 egg
4 cups grated potatoes
(6 medium potatoes)
½ cup grated onions

3 Tbsp. flour
½ tsp. salt
¼ tsp. pepper
3–4 Tbsp. oil or margarine

1. Beat egg, then mix in potatoes, onions, flour, salt and pepper.
2. Pour oil ⅛″ deep into a large skillet and heat until hot, but not smoking.
3. Shape 3 Tbsp. of dough into a patty. Place each in hot fat, flattening each with a spatula.
4. Fry for 2–3 minutes on each side till golden brown. Drain well on paper towels before serving.

An Apple Dumpling

2 big dippers of apples
1¼ lb. bread crumbs
3½ cups sugar
1 cup cream or milk

Dough

2 cups milk
2 cups water
4 eggs
2½ qts. flour

In saucepan combine apples, crumbs, sugar and milk. Cook until the apples are mushy. Drain and grind. Set aside.

Prepare dough by combining milk, water, eggs and flour. Roll out on floured board. Add filling and seal dough around it. Boil or steam as a regular dumpling.

An Apple Dumpling

Makes about 2 dozen dumplings

1 quart peeled, sliced apples	**Dough**
½ cup bread crumbs	**½ cup milk**
¾ cup sugar	**½ cup water**
3 Tbsp. cream	**2 eggs**
	5 cups flour

1. In a saucepan combine apples, crumbs, sugar and milk. Cook until the apples are mushy.
2. Drain and mash. Set aside.
3. Prepare dough by combining milk, water, eggs and flour.
4. Roll out on floured board to ⅛″ thickness. Cut into 5″ squares. Place 2–3 Tbsp. filling on each square and seal dough around it.
5. Boil in 4 inches of water for 5 minutes or steam in a steamer for 20 minutes.

Whey Dumpling

Whey Dumpling

8 lbs. whey or cottage cheese
1¼ lbs. bread crumbs or 3 qts.
16 eggs
¼ cup salt

¼ cup sugar
½ cup milk
2 cups flour (sometimes 4 cups)
½ cup dried onions

Dough

2½ cups water
2½ cups milk

3 eggs
3 qts. flour

Combine all ingredients for filling and set aside. Mix together all of the dough ingredients. Roll out on floured board. Add filling and seal dough around it. Deep fry until golden brown.

Whey Dumpling

Makes 20 dumplings

Filling

2 cups cottage cheese or whey	2 Tbsp. sugar
3 cups bread crumbs	⅛ cup milk
4 eggs	½ cup flour
1 pinch salt	⅛ cup dried onion

Dough

¾ cup water	3 cups flour
¾ cup milk	1 pinch salt
1 egg	baking powder (optional)

1. Combine all ingredients for the filling and set aside.
2. Mix together all of the dough ingredients.
3. Roll out on a floured board to ⅛″ thickness.
4. Cut into 5″ squares, fill each with one heaping Tbsp. filling and fold up corners. Seal.
5. Deep fry until golden brown.
6. Serve with hot syrup.

Waffles

7½ qts. flour   7¼ lbs. butter
7½ qts. milk   5 Tbsp. salt
60 eggs   5 Tbsp. baking powder
3 cups sugar

Beat butter until smooth. Add eggs. Mix together flour, salt, sugar and baking powder and stir in milk. Add to butter - egg mixture. Fry as usual.

Waffles

Makes 12 4" waffles

10¾ Tbsp. butter, softened
3 eggs
1½ cups flour
¼ tsp. salt

⅛ cup sugar
¾ tsp. baking powder
1½ cups milk

1. Cream butter until smooth.
2. Add eggs.
3. Mix together flour, salt, sugar and baking powder, then stir in milk.
4. Add to the butter-egg mixture.
5. Bake on a hot greased waffle iron until golden brown.

Meat Dumplings

2 to 3 qts. of meat
¾ lb. crumbs
2 Tbsp. salt and pepper mixed together

Dough

1½ qts. water
½ qt. rye flour
2 qts. white flour

Combine together meat, crumbs and salt and pepper. Set aside. Combine water, rye flour and white flour for the dough. Make each dumpling by stuffing 1 Tbsp. of dough with a small amount of the meat mixture. Drop on broth and simmer for 20 minutes. Do not lift lid while cooking.

Meat Dumpling

Makes 6 servings

Filling

4 cups cooked chicken or beef	¾ tsp. salt
¾ cup bread crumbs	¼ tsp. pepper

Dough

¾ cup water	1 cup white flour
¼ cup rye flour	

2 quarts meat broth

1. Combine meat, crumbs, salt and pepper. Set aside.
2. Combine the ingredients for the dough.
3. Roll out and cut into 2″ squares. Place 1 rounded tsp. of meat on each square of dough. Fold up each corner of the dough square and seal.
4. Drop into 2 quarts broth and simmer for 20 minutes. (Broth can be made by using beef bouillon cubes or using beef or chicken stock.)

French Toast

3 qt. bowl of eggs   ¼ cup sugar
3 qt. bowl of milk   2 cups flour
¼ cup salt   slices of bread

Combine eggs, milk, salt, sugar and flour. Dip slices of bread in mixture and fry like a pancake.

French Toast

Makes 8 slices

1 cup eggs   **1 Tbsp. sugar**
1 cup milk   **1 Tbsp. flour**
1 pinch salt   **8 slices bread**

1. Combine eggs, milk, salt, sugar and flour.
2. Dip slices of bread in mixture and fry on hot griddle
   like pancakes.

CAKES
—and—
ICINGS

Chocolate Roll

40 eggs, seperated
7½ cups sugar
1¼ cups cake flour
4 cups sifted flour
2½ cups cocoa

½ tsp. baking powder
½ tsp. salt
10 tsp. vanilla
1¼ cups water

Beat egg whites until stiff. Fold in half of the sugar, gradually. Beat until thick and light. Slowly stir in water. Beat egg yolks until thick and light. Carefully fold egg yolk into egg white mixture and blend. Fold in flour, cocoa, salt, baking powder and the rest of the sugar (sifted together). Spread in prepared pans and bake at 375° for about 12 minutes. When cool, roll like a jelly roll after applying icing. Don't spread too thickly. Don't apply when hot or icing will disappr. 2½ qts. of dough to a pan makes 9 pans.

Chocolate Roll

Makes 1 cake roll

4 eggs, separated
¾ cup sugar
2 Tbsp. water
2 Tbsp. cake flour
½ cup sifted all-purpose flour

¼ cup cocoa powder
½ tsp. salt
1 tsp. baking powder
1 tsp. vanilla

1. Beat egg whites until stiff.
2. Fold in *half* of the sugar, gradually. Beat until light.
3. Slowly stir in water.
4. Beat egg yolks till thick and light.
5. Sift together flours, cocoa, salt, baking powder and rest of sugar. Stir in egg yolks. Fold into batter. Fold in vanilla.
6. Spread in greased and floured jelly roll pan. Bake at 375° for 12 minutes.
7. Cool for a few minutes. Turn out onto towel, then, starting with the narrow end, roll cake up with towel. Set aside until completely cool.
8. Unroll cake and spread with icing (see page 74). Roll up and chill. Slice carefully and serve.

Icing for Chocolate Roll

5 cups margarine
5 cups sugar
10 tsp. vanilla
2½ cups flour
6 cups milk

Cook flour and milk until thick. Cool. Combine with margarine and sugar which have been creamed together. Add vanilla. Beat until nice spreading consistency.

Icing

¼ cup milk
⅔ cup flour
½ cup margarine, softened

½ cup sugar
1 tsp. vanilla

1. Cook flour and milk until thickened. Cool.
2. Cream margarine and sugar. Add to the milk mixture. Add 1 tsp. vanilla.
3. Cool. Spread on top of cooled chocolate cake.

Fudge Icing for Rolls

6¾ lbs. sugar
3¾ cups cream
2¼ cups butter

Mix all ingredients together and pour in pan before laying in rolls to bake. Flip rolls after baking to get fudge icing on the top.

Fudge Icing for Rolls

For one pan of rolls

¾ lb. sugar   ¼ cup butter, softened
¼ cup plus 2½ Tbsp. cream

1. Mix all ingredients together and pour into pan before placing rolls into pan to bake.
2. Flip rolls after baking so that fudge icing is on top.

Jelly Rolls

80 eggs
20¼ cups sugar
20¼ cups sifted flour

2¼ tsp. salt
20¼ tsp. baking powder
2 tsp. vanilla

Separate egg yolks from eggs. Cream yolks until fluffy. Add sugar, flour, salt and baking powder. Fold in stiffly beaten egg whites and vanilla. Pour into well-greased pans. Spread evenly ¼ inch thick. Bake at 350° for about 8 to 10 minutes. (When adding flour, also add egg whites at the same time, otherwise it gets too thick and hard to beat.)

Jelly Rolls

Makes one cake roll

4 eggs
1 cup sugar
1 cup sifted flour

⅛ tsp. salt
1 tsp. baking powder
½ tsp. vanilla

1. Separate egg yolks from whites.
2. Cream yolks until fluffy. Beat whites until stiff.
3. Add sugar, flour, salt and baking powder to yolks.
4. Immediately fold in stiffly beaten egg whites and vanilla.
5. Line jelly roll pan with aluminum foil or waxed paper. Grease this and pour batter into it. Spread evenly, to ¼″ thickness.
6. Bake at 350° for about 12-15 minutes.
7. Let cool in pan a few minutes, then turn out onto a towel and remove paper. Starting with the narrow end, roll up with the towel. Set aside until completely cool.
8. Unroll, spread with favorite jelly, roll again and chill. Slice carefully and serve.

Banana Cake

3¾ qts. sugar
3¼ lbs. margarine
26 eggs
3½ cups sour milk
4¼ Tbsp. baking soda (in milk)

6½ Tbsp. baking powder (in flour)
24 cups flour or 6 qts.
3½ Tbsp. vanilla
16 cups mashed bananas

Cream together butter and sugar. Add eggs, well beaten. Add flour and milk alternately. Last, add bananas. Bake at 300° for 25 to 30 minutes.

Banana Cake

Makes a 9" square cake or a 4" x 9" loaf cake

½ cup butter, softened
½ cup sugar
1 egg
1 tsp. baking powder
1¾ cups flour

½ tsp. baking soda
½ cup sour milk
1 tsp. vanilla
2 mashed bananas

1. Cream together butter and sugar.
2. Add beaten egg.
3. Mix baking powder and flour together.
4. Stir baking soda into milk.
5. Add flour mixture and milk alternately to creamed mixture, stirring as little as possible.
6. Fold in the vanilla and bananas.
7. Pour into greased cake pan. Bake at 350° for 30 minutes or until cake pulls away from pan.

Carrot Cake

20 cups flour
20 cups sugar
10 cups nuts
10 cups corn oil
30 cups grated carrots

20 tsp. baking soda
20 tsp. baking powder
20 tsp. vanilla
10 tsp. salt
40 eggs

Cream together oil and sugar. Add eggs, one at a time and beat again until creamy. Set aside. Mix dry ingredients together and add to batter, beating again until creamy. Add carrots and nuts. Mix until nice and even. Bake at 300° for 25 to 30 minutes. 3 lbs to a pan makes 17 pans.

Carrot Cake

Makes one 9" x 13" cake or 2 (4" x 7") loaf cakes

½ cup corn oil
1 cup sugar
2 eggs
2 cups flour
½ tsp. baking soda

1 tsp. baking powder
½ tsp. salt
1½ cups grated carrots
½ cup nuts
1 tsp. vanilla

1. Cream together oil and sugar.
2. Add eggs, one at a time, beating after each addition until creamy. Set aside.
3. Mix dry ingredients together and add to batter, stirring as little as possible.
4. Fold in carrots, nuts and vanilla.
5. Bake at 350° for 35 minutes or until a toothpick comes clean when inserted in middle of cake.

Carrot Cake Icing

5½ cups milk
5½ cups sugar
2¾ cups butter
17 egg yolks

2½ cups nuts
2½ cups shredded coconut
3 Tbsp. vanilla

Put milk, sugar, butter, and egg yolks together to cook. Let cook for 15 minutes. Cool. Add nuts, coconut and vanilla. Beat together for about 5 minutes.

Carrot Cake Icing

Makes icing for one 9" x 13" cake

⅔ cup milk
⅔ cup sugar
⅓ cup butter
2 egg yolks

¼ cup nuts
¼ cup shredded coconut
1 Tbsp. vanilla

1. Mix milk, sugar, butter and egg yolks together in saucepan.
2. Simmer for 15 minutes. Cool.
3. Add nuts, coconut and vanilla.
4. Beat together for about 5 minutes until completely cool, then spread on the cooled carrot cake.

Queen Elizabeth Cake

20 cups boiling water
15 cups chopped nuts
20 cups sugar
2½ lbs. margarine
20 tsp. baking powder
20 eggs, well beaten
20 tsp. vanilla
30 cups sifted flour
20 tsp. baking soda
10 cups dates
5 tsp. salt

Add soda to dates. Pour on boiling water and leave to cool overnight. Set aside. Cream together butter and sugar. Add vanilla and salt. Add nuts, baking powder and flour. Bake at 300° for one hour. 3¼ lbs. to each pan. This makes 16 pans.

Queen Elizabeth Cake

Makes one 9" square cake

1 tsp. baking soda
½ cup chopped dates
1 cup boiling water
3 Tbsp. butter or margarine
1 cup sugar
1 egg, well beaten

1 tsp. vanilla
1½ cups sifted flour
¼ tsp. salt
1 tsp. baking powder
¾ cup chopped nuts

1. Add baking soda to dates; pour boiling water over. Let stand to cool. Blend with mixer until mushy.
2. Cream together butter and sugar. Blend in egg.
3. Add vanilla.
4. Add flour, salt, baking powder and nuts. Stir in dates.
5. Bake at 350° for 20 minutes or until toothpick comes clean.

Angel Food Cake (Never Fail)

18 cups flour (super fine)   22½ cups egg whites
7½ tsp. salt   ½ cup cream of tartar
15 cups cake flour   ½ cup almond extract
15 cups powdered sugar

Sift first 3 ingredients twice and set aside. Beat egg whites, cream of tartar and almond extract on high speed. Add sugar, small amounts at a time. Carefully fold in flour mixture with a spatula. Bake from 30 to 40 minutes at 300°.

Variation: Use jello for flavoring instead of almond extract.

Angel Food Cake (Never Fail)

Makes one tube cake

1¼ cups cake flour	1½ tsp. cream of tartar
1 cup powdered sugar	1½ tsp. almond extract
¼ tsp. salt	(or 4 Tbsp. any flavor
½ cup egg whites	dry gelatin)
(from about 10 eggs)	¾ cup granulated sugar

1. Sift first three ingredients together twice. Set aside.
2. Beat egg whites, cream of tartar and almond extract (or dry gelatin) on high speed until mixture holds peaks. Add granulated sugar, small amounts at a time, folding it in carefully.
3. Gently fold in sifted ingredients, small amounts at a time.
4. Pour into an ungreased tube pan. Cut through batter once with a knife to eliminate bubbles.
5. Bake at 375° for 30 minutes. Invert to cool. Remove from pan.

Angel Food Cake

20 boxes of mix prepared according to directions on box.

Icing for Angel Food Cake

2 cups egg whites　　*14 cups powdered sugar*
6 cups syrup　　　　*1 Tbsp. salt*
1 cup sugar　　　　 *2 Tbsp. vanilla*

Add salt to egg whites and beat until stiff. Slowly add sugar. When stiff, slowly add syrup and vanilla. Add powdered sugar. Ready to spread.

Angel Food Cake

1 box of angel food cake mix prepared according to directions.

Icing for Angel Food Cake

½ cup egg whites　　　　　1½ cups corn syrup
¼ tsp. salt　　　　　　　 ½ tsp. vanilla
¼ cup sugar　　　　　　　3½ cups powdered sugar

1. Add salt to egg whites and beat until stiff.
2. Slowly add sugar.
3. When stiff, slowly add syrup and vanilla.
4. Add powdered sugar. Spread on cake.

Cherry Cake Frosting

1½ lbs. margarine
9 cups powdered sugar
4½ Tbsp. vanilla
1 cup milk
½ tsp. red food coloring

Beat margarine until softened. Add powdered sugar and stir in vanilla, milk and coloring. Beat until smooth and spreading consistency. Spread atop Duncan Hines cherry cake made from mix.

Cherry Cake Frosting

¾ lb. margarine, softened
4½ cups powdered sugar
1 tsp. vanilla

½ cup milk
few drops of red food coloring

1. Beat margarine until creamy.
2. Add powdered sugar, then stir in vanilla, milk and coloring.
3. Beat until smooth and of spreading consistency.
4. Spread atop Duncan Hines cherry cake made from a mix.

White Cake Icing

¾ lb. butter
1¼ cups cream
2 qts. powdered sugar

½ cup flour
½ cup cornstarch
½ Tbsp. vanilla

Beat butter until softened. Add cream. Add sugar, flour, cornstarch and vanilla. Beat until smooth and spreading consistency.

White Cake Icing

¼ lb. plus 2⅔ Tbsp. butter
⅔ cup cream
4 cups powdered sugar

¼ cup flour
¼ cup cornstarch
1 tsp. vanilla

1. Beat butter until softened.
2. Add cream and beat until smooth.
3. Add sugar, flour, cornstarch and vanilla. Beat until smooth and of spreading consistency.

Cream Cheese Frosting from Molly Wurtz

3 oz. cream cheese
1 tsp. vanilla
¼ cup margarine
powdered sugar

Mix cream cheese, vanilla and margarine until creamy and smooth. Add powdered sugar until it is just right for spreading. Enough for a 9 x 12 inch cake.

Cream Cheese Frosting from Molly Wurtz

Makes frosting for one 9" x 13" cake

3 ozs. cream cheese, softened   **¼ cup margarine, softened**
1 tsp. vanilla   **powdered sugar**

1. Mix cream cheese, vanilla and margarine until creamy and smooth.
2. Add powdered sugar until it is just right for spreading.

Cooked Marshmallow Icing

8 cups sugar
3 cups water
6 Tbsp. corn syrup

6 egg whites
36 marshmallows
6 tsp. vanilla

Cook sugar, water and corn syrup together until the mixture forms a soft ball when tested in cold water. Set aside. Beat egg whites until stiff. Add marshmallows. Pour syrup mixture slowly into egg-marshmallow mixture, beating constantly. Add vanilla. Beat until it is right consistency for spreading.

Cooked Marshmallow Icing

Makes frosting for one 9" x 13" cake

1⅓ cups granulated sugar	**1 egg white**
½ cup water	**6 large marshmallows**
1 Tbsp. corn syrup	**1 tsp. vanilla**

1. Cook sugar, water and corn syrup together until the mixture forms a soft ball when tested in cold water. Set aside.
2. Beat egg white until stiff.
3. Add marshmallows.
4. Pour syrup mixture slowly into egg-marshmallows mixture, beating constantly.
5. Add vanilla.
6. Beat until it is the right consistency for spreading.

Brownies

3½ lbs. butter
6¼ lbs. sugar
2¼ Tbsp. vanilla
27 eggs

7¾ cups flour
2 cups Hershey's cocoa
1 tsp. salt
6 cups chopped walnuts

Cream together butter and sugar. Add vanilla and eggs. Set aside. Sift together flour, cocoa and salt. Add to creamed mixture. Blend well. Add nuts. Bake in greased pans at 300° for 25 to 30 minutes. Cool before removing from pans.

Brownies

Makes one 9" x 13" pan

¾ cup plus 1 Tbsp. butter,
    softened
1½ cups sugar
1 tsp. vanilla
4 eggs

1 cup flour
¼ cup cocoa powder
¼ tsp. salt
¾ cup chopped walnuts

1. Cream together butter and sugar.
2. Add vanilla and eggs. Set aside.
3. Sift together flour, cocoa and salt.
4. Add to creamed mixture. Blend well. Stir in nuts.
5. Bake in greased pan at 300° for 25–30 minutes.
6. Cool before removing from pans.

These brownies are light and cakey, not chewy.

Food Patterns
Among the Hutterites

Hutterite food patterns reflect a unique blend of community-style cooking, German ethnic food traditions and North American influences. Menus are repeated throughout the year on a weekly basis with certain foods served on a daily schedule. While sauerkraut, noodles and sausage are common and popular menu items, Hutterite cooks also serve foods like spaghetti, pizza, Shake and Bake Chicken and Wheaties.

Among the Schmiedeleut in South Dakota, certain foods are usually served on a particular day of the week. Customarily, pies and cakes are baked and served on Tuesdays, but the main baking day is Thursday. Two women assigned to the task for one week decide what to make. The fanciest desserts appear at the Thursday noon meal. Bread-baking happens on Monday, Wednesday and Friday. Delicious homemade buns are baked on Saturday and served throughout the weekend. Whenever the supply of homemade bread is depleted, commercial bread takes its place.

Menus change with the seasons. During the summer and fall months, when fresh garden produce is available, canned or frozen foods are never served. Tossed salads and various dishes made with raw or cooked fresh vegetables grace the tables. Heavier foods such as duck, beef, potatoes and rich creamy desserts appear during planting and harvesting season when the workload is at its peak. Such foods are served much less frequently in the wintertime.

During the winter and early spring months the hours spent canning and preserving food begin to pay off. Canned vegetables often are simply heated with a bit of soup stock. Immediately after the fall potato harvest and sausage-making day, potato and sausage soup and potato dumplings become regular features. Commonly served only at the noon meal, soup is a popular winter dish. At all meals year-round a variety of pickles, relishes and salad dressings are available. Coffee, tea and unhomogenized milk are the main beverages. Children generally are not permitted to drink coffee and tea.

Like many of their North American neighbors, Hutterites have become more health-conscious in recent years. The Schmiedeleut Sunset Colony, in particular, has instituted some significant dietary changes. Little salt is used in cooking. Cream is no longer added to vegetables and many other dishes as a matter of course. Menus have been adjusted to include foods that help control cholesterol levels. While food traditions vary from colony to colony and from Leut to Leut, most Hutterites share a community-style cooking tradition passed down from their European forebears and influenced by their lives as North American citizens.

Eva Rose's Brownies from Chocolate Syrup

4 lbs. margarine
16 cups white sugar
64 eggs

10 lbs. chocolate syrup
16 cups white flour
nuts

Cream together margarine and white sugar. Add eggs and chocolate syrup. Add flour and nuts. Bake in greased pan for 25 to 35 minutes at 350°.

Eva Rose's Brownies From Chocolate Syrup

Makes one 9" x 13" pan

¼ lb. margarine, softened
1 cup sugar
4 eggs

1 cup chocolate syrup
1 cup flour
¾ cup chopped nuts

1. Cream together margarine and sugar.
2. Add eggs and chocolate syrup.
3. Add flour and nuts.
4. Bake in greased pan at 350° for 25–35 minutes.

These are a little more moist than other brownies.

Chocolate Icing

¾ lb. butter
1¼ cups cream
2 qts. powdered sugar
½ cup flour

½ cup cornstarch
½ Tbsp. vanilla
2 cups Hershey's cocoa

Beat butter until softened. Add cream. Add sugar, flour, cornstarch and vanilla. Add cocoa. Beat until smooth and spreading consistency.

Chocolate Icing

Icing for one 9" x 13" cake

¼ lb. butter
⅓ cup cream
2 cups powdered sugar
2 Tbsp. flour

2 Tbsp. cornstarch
1 tsp. vanilla
½ cup cocoa powder

1. Beat butter until softened. Add cream.
2. Blend in sugar, flour, cornstarch and vanilla.
3. Add cocoa. Beat until smooth and of spreading consistency.

New Frosting Recipe

2½ lbs. syrup   ½ Tbsp. salt
1¼ lbs. margarine   ⅛ cup vanilla
6¼ lbs. powdered sugar 2½ cups lukewarm water

Beat margarine until softened. Add other ingredients.
Beat until smooth and spreading consistency.

New Frosting Recipe

Frosting for one 9" x 13" cake

¼ lb. margarine   ½ tsp. salt
1 cup sugar   1 tsp. vanilla
1¼ lbs. powdered sugar   ½ cup lukewarm water

1. Beat margarine until softened.
2. Add other ingredients.
3. Beat until smooth and of spreading consistency.

Icing from the Bakery

4½ lbs. powdered sugar   1 tsp. salt
1½ lbs. shortening   ½ cup cornstarch
½ cup corn syrup   vanilla to taste
1 cup milk

Mix everything together and beat until smooth and creamy.

Icing from the Bakery

Icing for one 9" x 13" cake

1 lb. powdered sugar   ¼ tsp. salt
⅔ cup shortening   2 tsp. cornstarch
1½ Tbsp. corn syrup   vanilla to taste
¼ cup milk

Mix everything together and beat until smooth and creamy.

''I like this one best, but sometimes the women pick another one for cake as they want to.''—Head Cook

Butter Cream Icing from Clara at Glendale Colony

23 lbs. powdered sugar
5 lbs. shortening
2 Tbsp. salt
1 Tbsp. vanilla
3½ lbs. water

Cream together 1 lb. powdered sugar, shortening, salt and vanilla. Add 2 lbs. water and 22 lbs. powdered sugar, mix well. Add 1½ lbs. water and beat again.

Butter Cream Icing
from Clara at Glendale Colony

1 lb. powdered sugar   **½ tsp. vanilla**
¼ cup plus 2½ Tbsp. shortening   **¼ cup water**
¼ tsp. salt

1. Cream together ¼ lb. powdered sugar, shortening, salt and vanilla.
2. Add half of the water and rest of the powdered sugar. Mix well.
3. Add rest of the water and beat again until of spreading consistency.

Fudge Icing for Rolls

6¾ lbs. brown sugar
¾ cup cream
2¼ cups margarine

Let all ingredients boil until a sample looks like toffee when dropped in cold water. Pour over rolls.

Fudge Icing for Rolls

For one 9" x 13" pan of rolls

1⅓ lb. brown sugar　　　　　**½ cup butter (not margarine)**
2¾ cup thick cream

Let all ingredients come to a gradual boil on a low burner until a sample looks like toffee when dropped in cold water. Pour over rolls.

Icing for Wedding Cake

2 cups sugar   2 egg whites
⅓ cup corn syrup   1 tsp. vanilla
⅓ cup water

Cook together sugar, syrup and water until it spins a thread, about 3 minutes. Have ready stiffly whipped egg whites. Pour hot syrup slowly into egg whites, beating constantly. Add vanilla and beat until mixture is almost cool and is creamy to the taste and will hold shape when spreading a cake. This will frost a three layer cake with the lower layer weighing 4 lbs., the middle layer 3 lbs. and the top layer 2 lbs.

Icing for Wedding Cake

This will frost a 3-layer cake

2 egg whites	**⅓ cup water**
2 cups sugar	**1 tsp. vanilla**
⅓ cup corn syrup	

1. Beat egg whites until stiff. Set aside.
2. Cook sugar, syrup and water together until it spins a thread, about 3 minutes.
3. Pour hot syrup slowly into egg whites, beating constantly.
4. Add vanilla and beat until mixture is almost cool and creamy and holds its shape when spreading on cake.

Powered Sugar and Syrup Icing

3 cups egg whites   1 tsp. salt
6 cups white syrup   15 cups powdered sugar
¾ cup vanilla

Beat egg whites until stiff. Add salt. Slowly add syrup. When nice and fluffy, add powdered sugar and vanilla.

Powdered Sugar and Syrup Icing

Icing for rolls, pie or cream puffs

½ cup egg whites   1 tsp. vanilla
pinch of salt   2½ cups powdered sugar
1 cup light corn syrup

1. Beat egg whites until stiff.
2. Add salt.
3. Slowly add syrup.
4. When fluffy, add powdered sugar and vanilla.

Marshmallow Syrup Icing for Pies

1 cup powdered sugar   6 cups syrup
1 cup sugar   ½ Tbsp. salt
2 cups egg whites   ½ Tbsp. vanilla

Add salt to egg whites and beat until stiff. Slowly add sugar. When again stiff, add syrup and vanilla. Beat until nice and fluffy.

Marshmallow Syrup Icing for Pies

This syrup contains no marshmallows but tastes like it does.

⅛ tsp. salt   ¼ cup granulated sugar
½ cup egg whites   1½ cups light corn syrup
¼ cup powdered sugar   ¼ tsp. vanilla

1. Add salt to egg whites and beat until stiff.
2. Blend sugars together, then slowly add to egg whites, beating until sugars are absorbed and mixture is stiff.
3. Beat in syrup and vanilla until fluffy.

Pineapple Butter Frosting

2 lbs. margarine
4 lbs. powdered sugar
1 Tbsp. salt

4 egg yolks
24 oz. can of crushed pineapple
(drained)
2 Tbsp. vanilla

Cream together margarine, powdered sugar, salt and egg yolks until light and fluffy. Add pineapple and vanilla. Beat until nice and smooth.

Pineapple Butter Frosting

Frosting for one 9" x 13" cake

½ lb. margarine, softened
1 lb. powdered sugar
½ tsp. salt
1 egg yolk

6 ozs. crushed pineapple
(drained)
1 tsp. vanilla

1. Cream together margarine, powdered sugar, salt and egg yolk until light and fluffy.
2. Add pineapple and vanilla, beating until smooth.

Frosting for Brownies

9 cups sugar
1 cup and 2 Tbsp. cocoa
2 cups milk
2 cups butter

Mix all ingredients together and boil for 1 minute. Make sure it is a rolling boil. Beat until thick. Spread.

Frosting for Brownies

Frosting for 1 pan of brownies

2¼ cups granulated sugar   **½ cup milk**
½ cup cocoa powder   **½ cup butter**

1. Mix all ingredients together and boil for 1 minute at a rolling boil.
2. Beat until thickened. Spread on brownies.

Chocolate Syrup

10 cups cocoa   2 Tbsp. salt
12 cups hot water   4 Tbsp. vanilla
14 cups sugar

Mix together all ingredients and cook for 5 minutes, stirring until smooth. Remove from heat and add vanilla. Pour into jars while hot and cover tightly.

Chocolate Syrup

Makes about one pint

1 cup cocoa powder   **¼ tsp. salt**
1 cup plus 3 Tbsp. hot water   **1 tsp. vanilla**
1¼ cups sugar

1. Mix together all ingredients except vanilla and cook for 5 minutes, stirring until smooth.
2. Remove from heat and add vanilla.
3. Pour into a jar while hot and cover tightly.

DESSERTS
—and—
CANDY

Whip Cream Marshmallow Dessert

Crust
48 graham crackers, crushed
1½ cups melted butter
1¼ cups sugar

Mix together and press into pans. Prepare filling.

Filling
113 marshmallows
2¼ cups milk
7½ cups whipped cream
2¼ cups chocolate chips

Put marshmallows and milk in double boiler to soften. Cool and add whipped cream and chocolate chips. Blend well. Pour into crust. Cool before serving. Always whip cream at medium speed.

Whipped Cream Marshmallow Dessert

Makes 6 servings

Crust
16 graham crackers, crushed   **⅓ cup sugar**
½ cup butter, melted

Mix together and press into pan.

Filling
38 large marshmallows   **2½ cups heavy cream, whipped**
¾ cup milk   **¾ cup chocolate chips**

1. Heat marshmallows and milk in double boiler until marshmallows melt.
2. Cool and fold in whipped cream and chocolate chips, blending well.
3. Pour into crust. Cool before serving.

Strawberry Parfait Ring

2 cups sugar
⅔ cup water
1 drop red food coloring

24 egg whites
6 tsp. vanilla and a little salt
6 cups whipped cream

Beat egg whites until stiff, gradually adding hot syrup mixture which has been prepared by boiling sugar, water and food coloring for about 2½ minutes. Continue beating until cool. Add vanilla and salt. Fold in whipped cream and pour into bowls. Top with strawberries and freeze.

Strawberry Parfait Ring

Makes 6 servings

8 egg whites	**pinch of salt**
⅔ cup sugar	**2 cups heavy cream, whipped**
3 Tbsp. water	**2 (10 oz.) pkgs. frozen**
½ drop red food coloring	**strawberries or 2½ cups**
1 tsp. vanilla	**fresh strawberries, chopped**

1. Beat egg whites until stiff.
2. Boil sugar and water and food coloring mixture for about 2½ minutes.
3. Add gradually to the beaten egg whites, beating continually until cool.
4. Fold in vanilla and salt.
5. Fold in whipped cream and pour into parfait glasses. Top with strawberries and freeze.

Variations:
1. The strawberries may be added to the mixture, poured into a 9″ x 13″ cake pan and frozen. Cut in squares and serve.
2. One-half of the recipe fills 6 sherbet glasses. Pour strawberries on top and freeze.

Whipped Cream Dessert

2 cups rice, cooked
and drained
2 lbs. raisins
1 qt. pineapple

1 qt. whipped cream
2 cups sugar
1 Tbsp. vanilla

Mix together rice, raisins, pineapple, sugar and
vanilla. Fold in whipped cream.

Whipped Cream Dessert

Makes about 4 servings

1 cup cooked rice, drained
½ cup raisins
1 cup crushed pineapple,
drained

½ cup sugar
1 tsp. vanilla
1 cup heavy cream, whipped

1. Mix together rice, raisins, pineapple, sugar and vanilla.
2. Fold in whipped cream.
3. Serve in sherbet dishes.

Another Whipped Cream Dessert

1 gallon fruit cocktail   2 cups sugar
2 packages marshmallows   1 Tbsp. vanilla
1 qt. whipped cream

Mix together fruit, marshmallows, sugar and vanilla. Fold in whipped cream.

Another Whipped Cream Dessert

Makes 6 servings

1 quart fruit cocktail (drained)   1 tsp. vanilla
1 cup miniature marshmallows   1 cup heavy cream, whipped
½ cup sugar

1. Mix together fruit, marshmallows, sugar and vanilla.
2. Fold in whipped cream.
3. Cool and serve.

Orange Dessert

24 cut up orange pieces 2 cups sugar
1 qt. pineapple 1 Tbsp. vanilla
1 qt. whipped cream

Mix together orange pieces, pineapple, sugar and vanilla. Fold in whipped cream.

Orange Dessert

Makes 6 servings

6 orange segments, cut up
1 cup pineapple chunks,
  drained

½ cup sugar
1 tsp. vanilla
1 cup heavy cream, whipped

1. Mix together orange pieces, pineapple, sugar and vanilla.
2. Fold in whipped cream.
3. Chill and serve.

Whipped Cream Marshmallow Dessert

2 cups rice,
  cooked and drained
2 lbs. raisins
2 lbs. marshmallows

1 qt. whipped cream
2 cups sugar
1 Tbsp. vanilla

Mix together rice, raisins, marshmallows, sugar and vanilla. Fold in whipped cream.

Whipped Cream Marshmallow Dessert

Makes 6 servings

1 cup cooked rice
1 cup raisins
2 cups miniature
  marshmallows

½ cup sugar
1 tsp. vanilla
1 cup heavy cream, whipped

1. Mix together rice, raisins, marshmallows, sugar and vanilla.
2. Fold in whipped cream.
3. Chill and serve.

Jello Rice Dessert

1 cup rice, cooked
   and drained
½ gallon pineapple
8 packages of Jello

1 qt. whipped cream
1½ cups sugar
1 Tbsp. vanilla

Prepare Jello according to package directions. Let
until slightly stiff. Fold in rice and pineapple.
Fold in whipped cream to which sugar and vanilla
has been added. Chill.

Jello Rice Dessert

Makes 6 servings

1 small pkg. cherry gelatin
1 cup cooked rice
2 cups crushed pineapple
   (drained)

1 cup heavy cream, whipped
6½ Tbsp. sugar
1 tsp. vanilla

1. Prepare gelatin according to package directions.
2. Let set until slightly stiff.
3. Fold in rice and pineapple.
4. Fold in whipped cream to which sugar and vanilla have been
   added.
5. Chill and serve.

Fudge Candy

2 cups white sugar   1 cup brown sugar
1 cup honey   1 cup cream
1 cup milk   ½ cup margarine

Melt margarine and mix everything together. Cook for ½ to 1 hour or until it forms taffy-like ball in cold water.

Fudge Candy

This is very apt to curdle unless cooked slowly on low heat.

½ cup butter (not margarine)   1 cup milk
2 cups white sugar   1 cup brown sugar
1 cup honey   1 cup cream (very thick)

1. Melt butter, then mix everything together.
2. Cook for 30 minutes to 1 hour or until mixture forms a taffy-like ball in cold water.
3. When slightly cool, pour into a buttered pan 5″ x 10″. Mark into 1″ squares. Separate when mixture is fully cool and set.

Rhubarb Crush

17 cups flour
15 cups brown sugar
19½ cups oatmeal

7 cups melted butter (3½ lbs.)
9 qts. rhubarb (cut up)
12 cups sugar

Mix together brown sugar, 15 cups flour, oatmeal and melted butter. Set aside. Mix together rhubarb, 2 cups flour and sugar. Press into the bottom of a pan 2½ cups of crust mixture. Add 1½ cups rhubarb mixture on top. Top with 2½ cups of crust mixture. Bake at 375 or 400° for 40 to 45 minutes. Makes 12 pans.

Rhubarb Crush

Makes one 9" x 13" pan

1 cup brown sugar	½ cup melted butter
1¼ cups flour	3 cups rhubarb, cut up
1⅓ cups oatmeal	1 cup granulated sugar

1. Mix together brown sugar, 1 cup of the flour, oatmeal and melted butter. Set aside.
2. Mix together rhubarb, ¼ cup flour and granulated sugar. Set aside.
3. Press half of crumb mixture in bottom of 9" x 13" pan.
4. Spread rhubarb over crumbs.
5. Sprinkle last half of crumb mixture over the rhubarb.
6. Bake at 350° for 45 minutes.

Apple Crisp

15 cups brown sugar
17 cups flour
19½ cups oatmeal
7 cups melted butter (3½ lbs.)
8 qts. apples

Mix together 15 cups flour, brown sugar, oatmeal and melted butter. Set aside. Mix together apples and 2 cups flour. Press into the bottom of a pan 2½ cups of the first mixture. Spread 1½ cups of the apple mixture on top. Add 2½ cups of the first mixture on top. Bake at 375° for 35 to 40 minutes. This makes 12 pans.

Apple Crisp

Makes one 9" x 13" pan

1⅛ cups flour	½ cup melted butter
1 cup brown sugar	8 apples, peeled and sliced
1⅓ cups oatmeal	½ cup flour

1. Mix together the 1⅛ cups flour, brown sugar, oatmeal and melted butter. Set aside.
2. Mix together apples and ½ cup of flour. Set aside.
3. Press half of the crumb mixture into the bottom of a 9" x 13" pan.
4. Spread the apples on top.
5. Sprinkle last half of the crumb mixture on top of the apples.
6. Bake at 350° for 35 minutes.

PIES

Graham Cracker Cherry Pie

9 packages graham crackers (crushed)
2¼ cups butter
2¼ cups sugar

Melt butter and add other ingredients. Press into pie pans.

Filling

6 8-ounce packages of cream cheese
9 Tbsp. lemon juice
8½ cups sweetened condensed milk
cherry pie filling

Beat cream cheese at medium speed with mixer. Add milk and lemon juice. Pour into graham cracker crust and top with cherry pie filling. Chill a few hours before serving.

Graham Cracker Cherry Pie

Makes one 9" pie

¼ cup butter   ¼ cup sugar
20 graham crackers or
    1½ cups crumbs

1. Melt butter and add crumbs and sugar.
2. Bake 10 minutes at 350°.

Filling

8-oz. pkg. cream cheese,   2 Tbsp. lemon juice
    softened   1 can cherry pie filling
2 cups sweetened condensed
    milk

1. Beat cream cheese at medium speed with mixer.
2. Add milk and lemon juice.
3. Pour into graham cracker crust.
4. Top with cherry pie filling.
5. Chill a few hours before serving.

Fresh Blueberry Pie

7½ qts. blueberries   2 Tbsp. salt
14 cups sugar   2½ cups lemon juice
¾ lb. cornstarch   ½ cup vinegar
1½ cups flour

Mix all ingredients as usual. Bake at 325° for 30 to 35 minutes.

Fresh Blueberry Pie

Makes one 9" double-crusted pie

4 cups blueberries	**2 Tbsp. lemon juice**
1 cup sugar	**1 Tbsp. vinegar**
3 Tbsp. cornstarch	**1 unbaked double-crust pie**
¼ tsp. salt	

1. Mix all filling ingredients together gently.
2. Pour into bottom crust of pie.
3. Cover with top crust and bake at 350° for 30–35 minutes.

Pie Crust

3 cups shortening   water
4 qts. flour   3 eggs
2 Tbsp. baking powder   2 Tbsp. vinegar
2 tsp. salt

Beat shortening until smooth. Stir in flour, baking powder and salt. Add water to which eggs and vinegar has been added.

Pie Crust

Makes 3 9" pie crusts

1 cup shortening   **1 egg**
2⅔ cups flour   **2 tsp. vinegar**
2 tsp. baking powder   **1 Tbsp. cold water**
½ tsp. salt

1. Beat shortening until smooth.
2. Stir in flour, baking powder and salt.
3. Gradually add water to which egg and vinegar have been added.
4. Cut liquids into the dry mixture with 2 knives.
5. Divide in half and roll out in 3 circles for 3 9" pie pans.

''Some of the women think this crust holds together better because it uses shortening instead of butter.''—Head Cook

Peach Pie

4½ gallon jars of canned peaches and drained peach juice
or
1¼ qts. water if using fresh peaches

2½ cups tapioca
1 cup cornstarch
2 cups lemon juice
few drops orange coloring

Boil together juice or water, tapioca, cornstarch, lemon juice and coloring. When thick add drained peaches and boil again. Cool. Fill pie shells. Makes 16 pies. Cover with crust and bake as usual.

Peach Pie

Makes 1 9-inch pie

5 cups canned peaches, drained, or fresh peaches (about 9 medium peaches)
⅓ cup water or peach juice
2½ Tbsp. tapioca
1 Tbsp. cornstarch

1 cup sugar, if using fresh peaches
2 Tbsp. lemon juice
1–2 drops of orange food coloring
1 unbaked double-crust pie

1. Boil together juice or water and tapioca, cornstarch, sugar (if needed), lemon juice and coloring.
2. When thickened, add drained peaches and boil again. Cool.
3. Fill unbaked pie shell.
4. Cover with crust and bake at 350° for 40 minutes.

Fresh Strawberry Pie

Fresh Strawberry Pie

3 qts. water
3 qts sugar
¾ lb. cornstarch
½ cup vanilla

¼ cup butter
few drops of red food coloring
30 cups fresh strawberries

Cook over medium heat, water, sugar and cornstarch until thick and clear. Cool. Add butter, vanilla and food coloring. Mix in strawberries and pour into baked pie shells and chill. Top with whipped cream and garnish with more berries.

Do not add the filling to the pie crust too early before serving. It will get soggy. This does not keep long, but is very good.

Fresh Strawberry Pie

Makes 1 9" pie

1 cup plus 3 Tbsp. water	**1 tsp. vanilla**
1 cup plus 3 Tbsp. sugar	**few drops of red food coloring**
3 Tbsp. cornstarch	**4 cups fresh strawberries**
1 tsp. butter, softened	**1 baked pie shell**

1. Cook water, sugar and cornstarch over medium heat until thickened and clear. Cool.
2. Add butter, vanilla and food coloring.
3. Mix in strawberries and pour into *baked* pie shell and chill.
4. Top with whipped cream and garnish with berries.

Note: Add the filling to the pie crust just before serving to prevent the crust from getting soggy.

Cherry Pie Filling

17 lbs. frozen cherries   ¾ lb. cornstarch
7 lbs. cherry juice   3½ lbs. sugar
2½ lbs. corn syrup

Thaw frozen cherries slowly. Drain juice. Add water if necessary to make 7 lbs. juice. Bring to a boil. Dissolve starch in some of the juice and add it to the mixture. Add a mixture of the sugar and syrup to the batch. Bring it to a boil until slightly thickened. Add cherries and mix thoroughly. For pie, put filling in raw crust and add top crust. Bake at 375° for 30 to 35 minutes.

Cherry Pie

Makes 1 9" pie

4 cups fresh or frozen red
  sour cherries
1 cup cherry juice
¼ cup corn syrup
1 cup sugar

2 Tbsp. cornstarch
¼ cup cold water
1 unbaked double-crust pie
  shell

1. Thaw berries if frozen. Drain and set aside.
2. Mix juice, syrup and sugar and heat until near boiling.
3. Dissolve cornstarch in cold water and stir gradually into hot syrup mixture. Bring to boil.
4. Add the drained cherries and mix thoroughly.
5. Bake at 375° for 30 minutes in an unbaked double crust.
6. Cool before serving.

Apple Pie

1⅛ gallon sugar
6 half gallon jars of apples
½ lb. cornstarch
1 cup flour

Mix all ingredients and bake in raw pie shell with top for 30 minutes at 300°.

Apple Pie

Makes 1 9" pie

2 cups sugar
4 cups canned unsweetened apples
3 Tbsp. cornstarch
1 Tbsp. flour

1 unbaked double-crust pie shell

1. Mix all filling ingredients together.
2. Pour into unbaked crust and cover with a top crust.
3. Bake at 300° for 30 minutes.

A Structured Life
with Moments of Freedom

Hutterite colonies operate within schedules and around planned events dictated primarily by the weather, the seasons and the needs of the colony. In many cases the division of labor follows traditional roles in which men do ''men's work'' and women do ''women's work.'' In a general sense, this means women do not operate heavy equipment in the fields or workshops while men do not cook, clean or do the laundry. There are, of course, exceptions to the rule. For example, a husband and father whose wife has a heavy week on the rotating colony schedule is expected to help her. By the same token, women take over some of the ''men's work'' at the height of the planting and harvesting seasons.

Women between the ages of 15 and 45 constitute most of the female work force. Head managerial positions for women include head cook and garden woman. The head cook is usually, but not always, the wife of the colony steward or boss. She oversees all cooking and serving of food. She makes out the grocery list for store-bought foods. She also arranges the other details of women's work related to the kitchen and cooking. Women are divided into pairs. Each pair helps the head cook for one week in the kitchen, followed by one week in the bakery. The head cook also assigns teams of women to various tasks during spring and fall kitchen cleaning.

The garden woman oversees the women who work in the garden. She is also usually the gardener's wife. Responsible for all the non-mechanical work in the garden, she works with the gardener to supervise planting, hoeing and harvesting. She also makes sure the kitchen is amply supplied with whatever fresh produce has ripened. She decides when to can and freeze foods. Together with the head cook, she plans how much should be preserved, based on the previous year's shortages and excesses.

Another important position held by a woman is the *kranke köchin*. This woman cooks for those with special needs, such as persons on special or restricted diets, those who are ill and those recovering from an illness or a hospital stay. She also cooks for women with new babies. For six weeks following the birth of her child, a new mother receives a special supply of food. The recipes in this cookbook labeled ''for women'' relate to this old custom. Examples of these foods include women's buns, women's pancakes and waffles, chicken noodle soup and chicken and dumplings. New mothers also get special supplies of sugar, coffee and tea. They may choose either to give the food away or to keep it.

Women over the age of 45 are relieved of gardening, baking and cooking chores. But they continue to be responsible for such tasks as canning, butchering, cleaning and the care of kindergarten children. Three older colony women conduct kindergarten classes for children between two-and-one-half and five years of age. All families with infant children are assigned a girl, from 11 to 15 years old, as a babysitter. This frees the mothers to help with regularly scheduled chores.

Freezing Apples for Pie

2 pails of cut up apples
¾ pail sugar

Mix together and freeze in containers.

Freezing Apples for Pie

**2 ice cream pails of peeled,
cut-up, raw apples**
¾ ice cream pail of sugar

Mix together and freeze in 1-quart plastic bags.

Fresh Apple Pie

1 stainless steel pail apples
1/3 stainless steel pail sugar or 3 quarts
1/2 box or 1/2 lb. cornstarch
2 cups lemon juice
1 1/2 cups vinegar

Soak apples in half of the sugar overnight. In the morning add the rest of the sugar, starch and, if the apples are sweet, add the lemon juice and vinegar. Put in raw pie shell and cover with crust. Bake as usual.

Fresh Apple Pie

Makes 1 9" pie

4 cups raw, peeled, sliced
  apples
2 cups sugar
2 Tbsp. cornstarch

2 Tbsp. lemon juice
1 Tbsp. vinegar
1 unbaked double-pie crust

1. Soak apples in half the sugar overnight.
2. In the morning add rest of sugar and cornstarch.
3. If the apples are sweet, add the lemon juice and vinegar.
4. Put in an uncooked pie shell and cover with the uncooked crust.
5. Bake at 350° for 45 minutes or until crust is golden brown and apples are tender.

Crust for Pie

1 lb. margarine
2 cups fat
12 cups flour
2 Tbsp. baking powder
1 tsp. salt
3 cups water
2 eggs
2 Tbsp. vinegar

Beat margarine and fat until nice and fluffy. Stir in flour, baking powder and salt. Last, add 3 cups water to which eggs and vinegar has been added.

Crust for Pie

Makes 2 9" pie crusts

**2 Tbsp. and 2 tsp. margarine,
  softened**
⅓ cup lard or shortening
2 cups flour
1 tsp. baking powder
¼ tsp. salt
¼ cup water
1 egg, beaten
1 tsp. vinegar

1. Beat margarine and shortening until fluffy.
2. Cut in the flour, baking powder and salt.
3. Mix together the water, egg and vinegar.
4. Stir into other ingredients until the mixture forms a ball.
   Divide into 2 balls.
5. Roll out on floured board, then fit into 2 9″ pie pans.

Cottage Cheese Pie

12 lbs. cottage cheese
45 eggs
8 cups sugar
2¾ cups flour
2¾ cups milk

¼ cup melted butter
¼ cup vanilla
3½ cups syrup
2 tsp. salt

Beat eggs separately. Set aside. Beat butter, cream and flour together. Mix all other ingredients together and mix until nice and creamy. Put in pie shell and bake at 300° for 40 minutes.

Cottage Cheese Pie

Makes 1 9" pie

3 eggs	¾ cup sugar
1 tsp. melted butter	1 tsp. vanilla
2 Tbsp. plus 2 tsp. cream	¼ cup syrup
2 Tbsp. plus 2 tsp. flour	¼ tsp. salt
12-oz. carton cottage cheese	1 unbaked pie shell

1. Beat eggs well with fork. Set aside.
2. Beat butter, cream and flour together.
3. Mix all other ingredients together until creamy. (The curds will not disappear.)
4. Pour into unbaked pie shell and bake at 350° for about 40 minutes. Garnish with nutmeg.

Sugar Pie

4 ½ qts. cream
¾ qt. milk
4 ½ qts. sugar
3 ¾ cups flour
9 eggs

Beat everything together, but do not overbeat.
9 pans. Bake at 300° for 45 to 50 minutes.

Sugar Pie

Makes 1 9" pie

2 cups thick cream	**½ cup plus 1 Tbsp. flour**
⅓ cup milk	**1 egg**
2 cups sugar	**1 unbaked pie shell**

1. Beat filling ingredients together gently without overbeating.
2. Pour into unbaked pie shell.
3. Bake for 45 minutes at 350°.

Butterscotch Pie

2½ qts. milk
1½ qts. brown sugar
¾ box cornstarch
1½ cups cold water

½ cup butter
20 egg yolks
2½ tsp. salt
⅛ cup vanilla

Mix crust as for other pies and bake. Cool. Bring milk to a boil. Dissolve cornstarch in cold water and add sugar. Combine with milk. After boiling for 3 minutes, add butter, yolks and salt. Boil for another minute. Cool. Add vanilla.

Butterscotch Pie

Makes 1 9" pie

1¾ cups milk
3 rounded Tbsp. cornstarch
3 Tbsp. cold water
¾ cup brown sugar
2 tsp. butter

2 egg yolks (reserve whites)
¼ tsp. salt
1 tsp. vanilla
1 baked 9" pie crust
4 Tbsp. granulated sugar

1. Bring milk to a boil.
2. Dissolve cornstarch in cold water and add sugar.
3. Combine with the hot milk.
4. After boiling 3 minutes, cool slightly, then add butter, yolks of eggs and salt.
5. Beat for another minute.
6. Cool. Add vanilla.
7. Pour into baked pie crust.
8. With electric beater, beat the egg whites until they form peaks.
9. Add 4 Tbsp. sugar and beat another 2 minutes.
10. Pour meringue over the pie and bake in 325° oven for 15 minutes or till golden brown. Cool.

Lemon Pie

2 cups lemon juice
3¾ qts. boiling water
¼ cup butter
2¾ cups sugar
¾ lb. cornstarch
½ cup flour
15 egg yolks

To 2 qts. boiling water add 1¾ qts. water to which cornstarch and flour has been combined. Add sugar slowly. Cook about 5 minutes. When almost done, add butter and egg yolks. Last, add lemon juice.

Lemon Pie

Makes 1 9" pie

2½ cups water
½ cup freshly squeezed lemon juice
3 Tbsp. cornstarch
4 Tbsp. flour
½ cup water

¾ cup sugar   Used   1 cup
2½ tsp. butter
2 egg yolks (reserve whites)
1 baked 9" pie shell
4 Tbsp. sugar

(handwritten: ⅓ c Cornstarch)

1. Bring 2½ cups water and ½ cup lemon juice to boil.
2. In separate bowl stir cornstarch and flour into ½ cup of water.
3. When water and lemon juice reach the boiling point, add the thickening, stirring slowly with wire beater.
4. Slowly add the sugar and boil 5 minutes.
5. When almost done, add butter and egg yolks.
6. Pour into 9-inch *baked* pie shell.
7. Beat the 2 egg whites till they form peaks, then add 4 Tbsp. sugar and beat again.
8. Spread meringue on the lemon pie and bake for 15 minutes at 350° or until meringue is golden brown. Cool.

Pumpkin Pie

2 gallons cooked pumpkin ½ cup vanilla
10 cups milk 10 cups sugar
24 eggs 1 heaping Tbsp. salt
1 cup flour

Mix pumpkin with milk and other ingredients. Pour into raw open pie crusts and bake slowly for 40 to 50 minutes. Pumpkin spice should be used on top.
Oven should be at 315°.

Pumpkin Pie

Makes 1 9" pie

2 cups cooked pumpkin
1 cup evaporated milk or
   half and half
1¼ cups sugar
3 eggs

1½ Tbsp. flour
2 tsp. vanilla
¼ tsp. salt
2 tsp. pumpkin pie spice
1 unbaked 9-inch pie shell

1. Mix pumpkin with milk and sugar.
2. Beat eggs slightly and add to the pumpkin mixture.
3. Add other filling ingredients. (Add the pumpkin pie spice to the mixture or sprinkle on top.)
4. Pour into an unbaked pie shell.
5. Bake for about 45 minutes at 350° or until a knife comes out clean.

Rhubarb Pie

1 stainless steel pail of rhubarb
½ pail sugar or 5 qts.
½ lb. cornstarch

Mix all ingredients together and let stand
overnight. You may reduce rhubarb by 4 qts. and
add 4 cups of raisins. Bake at 300° for 30 minutes.

Rhubarb Pie

Makes 1 9" pie

**4 cups fresh or frozen cut-up
rhubarb (½ inch pieces)
2 cups sugar**

**3 Tbsp. cornstarch
1 double unbaked 9-inch
pie crust**

1. Mix all filling ingredients together and let stand overnight.
2. Place in an unbaked pie shell and cover with a top crust and seal.
3. Bake at 425° for 10 minutes, then at 325° for 30 more minutes.

Banana Pie

3 qts. milk
3 cups sugar
1½ cups Karo syrup
6¼ tsp. vanilla

19 egg yolks
¾ box cornstarch
1½ tsp. salt

mix 2 qts. milk with syrup and sugar in top of double boiler. Dissolve cornstarch in 1¼ qts. milk and add to above mixture when it boils. Boil until it thickens and then add beaten egg yolks and vanilla. Pour into baked pie shell.

Banana Pie

Makes 1 9" pie

2 cups milk
¼ cup light corn syrup
½ cup sugar
3 Tbsp. cornstarch
3 eggs, separated

¼ tsp. salt
1 tsp. vanilla
1 cup sliced bananas
1 baked 9" pie shell

1. Mix 1½ cups milk with the syrup and sugar in top of double boiler.
2. Dissolve cornstarch in ½ cup milk and add to above mixture when it boils. Boil until it thickens and then add beaten egg yolks, salt and vanilla.
3. Cool, then pour into baked pie shell.
4. Cover with banana slices.
5. Beat the 3 egg whites until stiff. Pile lightly on top of pie. Bake till golden brown.

Chocolate Pie

4 qts. boiling water   1 box cornstarch
4 cups sugar   1½ cups dry chocolate
16 egg yolks   ¼ cup vanilla
1¼ cups butter

Put 2 qts. boiling water in a pan. Add cornstarch to one qt. water and stir in. When mixture is boiling, add sugar. Add chocolate which has been dissolved in 1 qt. water. When almost done, add butter and egg yolks. Last, add vanilla. Pour into baked pie shell.

Chocolate Pie

Makes 1 9" pie

3 cups boiling water   2 eggs, separated
3 Tbsp. cornstarch   1 tsp. vanilla
½ cup sugar   1 baked 9" pie crust
3 Tbsp. cocoa powder   4 Tbsp. granulated sugar
2 Tbsp. butter

1. Bring 2 cups water to a boil.
2. Add cornstarch to remaining 1 cup of water. Set aside.
3. When water boils, add sugar, the cornstarch mixture and cocoa powder.
4. When thickened, add butter and egg yolks.
5. Finally, add vanilla.
6. Pour into baked pie shell.
7. Beat egg whites till stiff and add 4 Tbsp. sugar. Beat again till stiff.
8. Spread on top of cooled pie and bake till meringue is golden brown.

Cream Pie

3 qts. milk
3 cups sugar
1 cup Karo syrup
4 tsp. vanilla

12 egg yolks
3/4 box cornstarch
1 tsp. salt

Mix 1½ qts. milk with syrup in top of double boiler. Dissolve cornstarch and sugar in rest of milk. When boiling, combine the two mixtures and cook for 3 minutes. When done, slowly add egg yolks. Add vanilla last.

Cream Pie

Makes 1 9-inch pie

3 cups milk
⅓ cup corn syrup
3 Tbsp. cornstarch
1 cup sugar
4 egg yolks (save whites)

¼ tsp. salt
1 tsp. vanilla
1 9-inch baked pie crust
4 Tbsp. granulated sugar

1. Mix 2 cups of milk with syrup. Begin to cook over low heat.
2. Dissolve cornstarch and sugar in rest of milk. Set aside.
3. When milk and syrup come to a boil, add the cornstarch mixture and cook for 3 minutes.
4. When done, slowly add egg yolks and salt.
5. Finally, add vanilla.
6. Pour into baked pie shell.
7. Beat the egg whites until they form peaks. Add 4 Tbsp. sugar and beat until stiff.
8. Bake until golden brown.

MEAT, FISH and MAIN DISHES

Brine for Sour Meat or Pickled Meat

¾ gallon water
¾ gallon vinegar
½ cup salt

1. Mix together all ingredients and let come to a full boil.
2. Pour onto pig's feet.
3. Allow to stand for 1 week.

Brine for Sour Meat or Pickled Meat

¾ gallon water
¾ gallon vinegar
½ cup salt

Mix together all ingredients and let boil over. Pour on pig's feet.

Buckwheat Sausage

1 qt. buckwheat
1¼ gallons water
1½ pails pork (pre-cooked and ground)
1 pail beef (pre-cooked and ground)

½ cup salt
¼ cup pepper
3 qts. water

Mix together all ingredients. Put into casings. Cool. When ready to serve, boil or roast for 15 minutes.

Buckwheat Sausage

1 qt. buckwheat
1¼ gallons water
1½ pails pork (pre-cooked and ground)
1 pail beef (pre-cooked and ground)

½ cup salt
¼ cup pepper
3 qts. water

1. Mix together all ingredients.
2. Put into casings. Cool.
3. When ready to serve, boil or roast for 15 minutes.

Liver Sausage

10 livers, fine ground, from hogs

1½ bushels of scraped hog skin or 6 pails

2 pig heads

1½ pails of scrap meat cut from bones

4 gallons soup made from above scrap meat

1 pan onions, fried and ground (1½ qts.)

1 cup salt

1 cup pepper

(This recipe includes 6 pails of meat, altogether)

Precook all meat. Mix together all ingredients and fill casings. Cool. When ready to serve, roast or boil for 15 minutes.

Heart Sausage

the hearts and tongues from hogs
3 pails of hog meat
1 cup salt
¾ cup pepper
2 to 3 gallons of garlic water
(3 Tbsp. garlic)

Precook and grind all meat. Mix together all ingredients and put into casings. Cool. When ready to serve, roast or boil for 15 minutes.

Heart Sausage

One pork heart and one tongue
½ pail hog meat
¼ cup salt

⅛ cup pepper
½ gal. water seasoned with
   1 Tbsp. garlic

1. Pre-cook and grind all meat.
2. Mix together all ingredients and put into casings. Cool.
3. When ready to serve, roast or boil for 15 minutes.

Small Baloney Recipe

15 lbs. hamburger
(precooked and ground)
10 lbs. beef meat
(precooked and ground)
7½ lbs. water

½ cup sugar
¼ cup salt
1 tsp. pepper
¼ cup tender quick

Mix together all ingredients and fill casings. Cool.
When ready to serve, boil or roast for 15 minutes.

Small Baloney Recipe

Makes 2 baloney rings

2 lbs. hamburger (pre-cooked
   and ground)
2 lbs. stewing beef (pre-cooked
   and ground)
3 cups water

5 tsp. sugar
2½ tsp. salt
⅛ tsp. pepper
2½ tsp. Tender Quick

1. Mix together all ingredients and fill casings. Cool.
2. When ready to serve, boil or roast for 15 minutes.

New Baloney Recipe

⅓ cup liquid smoke
30 lbs. pig meat
    (precooked and ground)
20 lbs. beef meat
    (precooked and ground)

15 lbs. water
¾ cup sugar
½ cup salt
1 Tbsp. pepper
½ cup tender quick

Mix together all ingredients and fill casings. Cool. When ready to serve, boil or roast for 15 minutes.

New Baloney Recipe

1 Tbsp. liquid smoke
3 lbs. pork (pre-cooked and
    ground)
2 lbs. beef (pre-cooked and
    ground)

2¼ cups plus 2½ Tbsp. water
3 Tbsp. sugar
2 Tbsp. salt
1 tsp. pepper
1 Tbsp. Tender Quick

1. Mix together all ingredients and fill casings. Cool.
2. When ready to serve, boil or roast for 15 minutes.

Baloney Recipe from Rockport Colony

100 lbs. meat (precooked and ground)
½ gallon hot water
1½ lbs. curing salt

½ cup pepper
12 oz. garlic salt
One handful coriander or ½ cup

Mix together all ingredients and fill casings. When ready to serve, boil or roast for 15 minutes.

Baloney Recipe from Rockport Colony

Rockport Colony is located in Hanson County which is in southeastern South Dakota near the James River.

Makes 4–5 rings

10 lbs. meat (pre-cooked and ground)
3 qts. plus ¾ cup hot water
⅛ lb. curing salt

1⅕ tsp. pepper
1 rounded Tbsp. garlic salt
½ tsp. coriander

1. Mix together all ingredients and fill casings.
2. When ready to serve, boil or roast for 15 minutes.

Liver

10 lbs. liver
1-2 qt. bowl of eggs
(if any)
2 cups flour

¼ cup mixed salt
1 qt. water or soup
½ qt. fat

Mix together liver, eggs, flour and mixed salt. add to 1 qt. water and ½ qt. fat. Cook in sauce pan until done. Fill casings. Cool. To serve, boil for 5 minutes in plain water.

Liver

1 lb. liver, ground	**1 tsp. mixed salt**
⅓ cup beaten eggs	**⅓ cup water or soup stock**
3 Tbsp. flour	**3 Tbsp. fat, melted**

1. Mix together liver, eggs, flour and mixed salt.
2. Add to water and fat.
3. Cook in saucepan until done.
4. Fill casings. Cool.
5. To serve, boil for 5 minutes in plain water.

Oven Hamburgers and Hotplate

30 lbs. hamburger meat   ¼ cup salt
6 lbs. water   1 tsp. pepper
½ cup sugar

Mix all ingredients together and put in oven at 9 a.m. or 10:30 a.m. Bake at 400° and then reduce to medium heat until done.

Oven Hamburgers and Hotplate

Makes 5–6 servings

1 lb. ground beef   **¼ tsp. salt**
3 Tbsp. water   **¼ tsp. pepper**
½ tsp. sugar

1. Mix all ingredients together. Shape into hamburgers.
2. Bake at 350° for 30 minutes.

Sauce for Meats and Ribs

1½ qts. tomato juice
1 qt. water
1½ cups cornstarch
1½ cups flour

½ cup sugar
½ cup soy sauce
½ cup Worcestershire sauce
¼ cup gravy coloring

Mix all ingredients and pour on hamburgers or ribs at 10:30 a.m.

Sauce for Meats and Ribs

Makes 1½ cups sauce

½ **cup tomato juice**	6 **tsp. sugar**
⅓ **cup water**	6 **tsp. soy sauce**
⅛ **cup cornstarch**	6 **tsp. Worcestershire sauce**
⅛ **cup flour**	3 **tsp. gravy coloring**

Mix all ingredients and pour on hamburgers or ribs about an hour before cooking.

Sauce for Sausage

1 qt. Russian dressing
½ qt. catsup
½ qt. tomato juice
3 Tbsp. cornstarch

Mix all ingredients. Heat. Pour over sausages.

Sauce for Sausage

Makes 2 cups

1 cup Russian dressing
½ cup catsup

½ cup tomato juice
2½ tsp. cornstarch

1. Mix all ingredients. Heat.
2. Pour over sausages.

Shake and Bake Coating Mix for Meat

4½ qts. dry measured
    bread crumbs
4 cups vegetable oil
4 Tbsp. salt
8 Tbsp. paprika

8 Tbsp. celery salt or seed
8 Tbsp. onion powder
parsley flakes (optional)

Mix all ingredients together. Dip meat in this coating mix and put meat in pans. Do not grease pans. Cover and bake at 300° until done.

Shake and Bake Coating for Meat

Makes about 5 cups

4 cups dry bread crumbs
¼ cup vegetable oil
¾ tsp. salt
1½ tsp. paprika

1½ tsp. celery salt or seed
1½ tsp. onion powder
parsley flakes (optional)

1. Mix all ingredients together.
2. Spoon coating mix over meat and place in ungreased baking pans.
3. Cover and bake at 300° until done.

Barbecue Sauce

2 cups catsup
4 Tbsp. worchestershire sauce
½ cup vinegar
2 tsp. salt
2 tsp. chili powder

2 cups water
1 tsp. celery seed
½ tsp. pepper
½ cup packed brown sugar

Mix all ingredients together. Boil. Pour over meat and bake.

Left over Chicken and Rice

5 cups rice
2½ onions, diced
4 cut-up chicken pieces

Cook and drain rice. Set aside. Fry onions in fat. Add chicken pieces and fry a little. Mix all ingredients together and spread ½ cup mayonnaise dressing on top. Add 2 Tbsp. salt. Bake in oven.

Left-over Chicken and Rice

Makes 6 servings

1 cup rice
½ cup onion, diced
2 Tbsp. oil

1 chicken, cut in pieces
½ cup mayonnaise
½ tsp. salt

1. Cook rice. Set aside.
2. Fry onions in oil. Add chicken pieces and brown.
3. Stir in rice.
4. Spread mayonnaise dressing over top.
5. Sprinkle with salt.
6. Bake at 350° for 1 hour.

Fish Burgers

3 cans mustard sardines   ½ qt. milk
3 cans catsup sardines   2 qts. ground chicken meat
2 cups mashed potatoes   (precooked)
10 eggs   salt and pepper
1 qt. bread crumbs

Mix together all ingredients. Fill sandwiches with mixture and cook slowly on grill until the filling is done and the bread is toasted.

Fish Burgers

Makes 6 servings

1 can mustard sardines
1 can catsup sardines
⅔ cup mashed potatoes
3 eggs
1⅓ cups bread crumbs
⅔ cup milk

2⅔ cups ground chicken meat
   (pre-cooked)
salt and pepper
12 slices of bread, buttered on
   one side

1. Mix together all filling ingredients.
2. Spread 6 slices of bread with mixture. Top with remaining 6 slices and cook slowly on grill, buttered side down, until the filling is done and the bread is toasted.

Sardine Sandwich

2 boxes fish of any kind
3 cooked eggs, boiled well done
3 cucumbers
3 spoons of dressing
a little pepper and salt

Mix all ingredients. Use as sandwich spread.

Sardine Sandwich

Makes 6 servings

1 can of sardines
2 cooked eggs, boiled hard
1 cucumber, chopped

1½ tsp. mayonnaise
dash pepper and salt

1. Mix all ingredients.
2. Spread on bread for sandwiches.

Hamburger Casserole

20 lbs. hamburger meat
2 qts. sliced potatoes
2 cups carrot pieces
2 cups onion pieces
2 cups celery pieces
½ qt. water
½ qt. tomato juice

Grease a casserole pan and line it with potatoes, carrots, onions and celery pieces until they are all used up. Salt to taste. Add hamburger on top. Pour over water and tomato juice. Let bake at 450° for 1½ hours.

Hamburger Casserole

Makes 4 servings

1 cup sliced potatoes
¼ cup carrot slices
¼ cup onion, chopped
1½ cups tomato juice
¼ cup celery pieces
dash salt
1 lb. hamburger
1½ Tbsp. water

1. Grease a casserole pan and line it with potatoes, carrots, onions and celery until used up.
2. Salt to taste.
3. Add hamburger on top and pour tomato juice and water over the top.
4. Bake for 1½ hours at 350°.

Spaghetti Meat Sauce

12 lbs. ground beef
1 cup salad oil
6 chopped onions
1 c. p. celery seed
1 jar tomato paste

1 jar tomato juice
1 tsp. cayenne pepper
1 tsp. curry powder
¼ cup salt
¼ cup chili powder

Brown ground beef and onions. Add other ingredients. Simmer.

Spaghetti Meat Sauce

Makes 6 servings

1 lb. ground beef
1 Tbsp. plus 1 tsp. salad oil
½ cup chopped onions
1 Tbsp. plus 1 tsp. celery seed
½ cup catsup

1 qt. tomato juice
1 tsp. chili powder
dash cayenne pepper
dash curry powder
1 tsp. salt

1. Brown ground beef and onions.
2. Add other ingredients.
3. Simmer for several hours.

Sample Menu for a Week
Sunset Colony, Schmiedeleut

MONDAY

Breakfast	Dinner	Supper
Cheese	Chicken, stuffed and roasted	Pizza
Oatmeal with milk	Potatoes with gravy	Shoestring potatoes, deep fried
Toast and butter	Sweet peas	Canned pears
	Bread	Bread
	Pickles	Relish

TUESDAY

Breakfast	Dinner	Supper
Commercial cereal with milk	Beef pieces in gravy	Wieners with buns
Toast and butter	Mashed potatoes	Baked potatoes
Cheese	Frozen corn, cooked	Sauerkraut
	Coleslaw	Canned peaches
	Relish	Pickles
	Bread	

WEDNESDAY

Breakfast	Dinner	Supper
Poached eggs	Swiss steak, fried and baked	Tuna casserole
Wieners or sausage	Mashed potatoes	Bean salad
Toast and butter	Boiled carrots	Canned cherries
	Whipped cream dessert or canned fruit	Bread
	Bread	

THURSDAY

Breakfast	Dinner	Supper
Canned fruit	Chicken soup with dumplings	Sausage
Cheese	Boiled potatoes	Baked potatoes
Toast and butter	Sauerkraut	Corn
	Canned peaches	Canned cherries
	Fresh baked bread	Fresh baked bread
	Rhubarb pie	

FRIDAY

Breakfast	Dinner	Supper
Commercial cereal	Boiled ham	Wieners in dough
Cheese and toast	Stringbean and potato cream soup	Bread
	Mustard stringbeans	Pickles
	Pickled cucumbers	Applesauce
	Bread	
	Doughnuts with jelly	

SATURDAY

Breakfast	Dinner	Supper
Hard-cooked egg	Turkey cutlets, coated and deep fried	Tuna fish
Boiled wiener or summer sausage	Boiled potatoes	Shoestring potatoes, deep fried
Toast	Buns	Boiled egg
		Buns
		Rhubarb with sugar

SUNDAY

Breakfast	Dinner	Supper
Boiled egg	Soup with chicken	Pressed ham and cheese
Summer sausage or canned fish	Boiled potatoes	Spaghetti with sauce
Buns and jelly	Buns	Cucumber salad
	Coleslaw	Canned apricots
	Beets (boiled or in vinegar)	Buns and jelly
	Cooked sauerkraut	

Tuna Spaghetti Casserole

2 lbs. spaghetti, cooked
and drained
6 6½-oz. cans of tuna
flaked and drained
1 cup chopped pimentos
4 Tbsp. margarine

4 10½-oz. cans of condensed
mushroom soup
2 cups milk
1 lb. grated cheese
2 cups crushed potato chips

Combine first three ingredients and set aside. In sauce pan, combine soup, milk and cheese. Heat and stir until cheese melts. Add tuna mixture and stir well. Pour into greased casserole and sprinkle with crushed potato chips. Bake at 350° for 30 minutes.

Tuna Spaghetti Casserole

Makes 6–8 servings

½ lb. dry spaghetti
1½ 6½-oz. cans tuna, flaked
and drained
¼ cup chopped pimentos
1 Tbsp. margarine

1 can cream of mushroom
soup
½ cup milk
4 ozs. grated cheese
½ cup crushed potato chips

1. Boil the spaghetti in boiling salted (2 tsp.) water for 8–10 minutes. Drain and cool.
2. Combine tuna, pimentos, margarine and spaghetti.
3. Warm soup, milk and cheese.
4. Add tuna mixture and stir well.
5. Pour into a 3-qt. greased casserole and sprinkle with crushed potato chips.
6. Bake at 350° for 30 minutes.

Chicken Pie Crust

3 cups shortening
4½ qts. flour
2 Tbsp. baking powder
2 tsp. salt

1¼ qts. water
2 eggs
2 Tbsp. vinegar

Beat shortening until smooth. Stir in flour, baking powder and salt mixture. Add water to which eggs and vinegar has been added.

Chicken Pie

Makes 2 8" pies

Crust

½ cup shortening
2 cups flour
1 tsp. baking powder
⅓ tsp. salt

2 Tbsp. water
1 egg
1 tsp. vinegar

1. Beat shortening until smooth.
2. Stir in flour, baking powder and salt.
3. Mix water, egg and vinegar together. Stir into batter with a fork until mixture forms a ball.
4. Roll out and place in pie pans or baking dishes.

Chicken Pie Filling

gravy
3 qts. chicken pieces
1 qt. cut-up potatoes

2 cups carrots
1 cup peas
1 cup celery, if any

Mix a gravy. Pour rest of ingredients into gravy. Stir well. Fill pie shells and cover with crust. Bake at 400° for 25 to 30 minutes or until golden brown.

Chicken Pie Filling

4 Tbsp. butter or margarine
4 Tbsp. flour
1 tsp. salt
2 cups chicken broth
1 raw potato, cubed

2 carrots, sliced
½ cup peas
2 stalks celery, chopped
2 cups cooked chicken pieces

1. Melt butter or margarine. Stir in flour and salt until smooth. Gradually add broth, stirring over low heat until thickened and smooth.
2. Partially cook the raw vegetables. Drain. Stir in cooked chicken.
3. Mix with gravy and fill the 2 pie shells.
4. Bake at 400° for 25–30 minutes or until golden brown.

Pizza Crust

1 qt. lard
1 Tbsp. salt
2 Tbsp. vinegar
3½ qts. flour
1 qt. water

or use regular bread dough

Pizza Crust

1¼ cups flour
⅓ tsp. salt
½ cup lard

¾ tsp. vinegar
½ cup water

1. Combine flour and salt.
2. Cut the lard into the flour and salt until mixture is crumbly.
3. Add the water and vinegar, stirring with a fork until the mixture forms a ball.
4. Divide ball in two. Roll out each ball between 2 sheets of waxed paper. Lift into pizza pans.

Pizza Pie

20 lbs. ground beef   6 tsp. salt
2 Tbsp. onion powder 4 tsp. chili powder
3 tsp. pepper   pizza sauce
3 tsp. paprika   cheese

Mix all ingredients together. Broil until done. Have the meat mixture ready and put 1½ cups on each pizza crust, add ¼ cup pizza sauce, and sprinkle with grated cheese. Bake at 400° until nice and brown.

Pizza Pie

Makes 2 11" pizzas. Each pizza makes 6 servings.

1½ lbs. hamburger
½ tsp. onion powder
¼ tsp. pepper
½ tsp. salt
½ tsp. chili powder

2 unbaked pizza crusts
1 cup pizza sauce
½ cup grated parmesan cheese
1 cup grated cheddar cheese
¼ tsp. paprika

1. Mix first 5 ingredients together.
2. Broil or brown in a skillet until hamburger is done.
3. Spread half of meat mixture on each crust.
4. Pour ½ cup pizza sauce over each pizza.
5. Sprinkle with grated cheeses and paprika.
6. Bake at 400° until crusts are golden brown.

Tomato Sauce for Macaroni

2 qts. tomato juice   ½ qt. Catalina dressing
¾ cup cornstarch   ½ qt. catsup
¾ cup sugar   1 Tbsp. salt

Mix all ingredients together and bring to a boil until it thickens. Pour over cooked macaroni.

This sauce may also be used over string beans. It is also good on onions which have been baked for ½ hour.

Tomato Sauce for Macaroni

Makes 6 servings

1 qt. tomato juice	**½ cup Catalina salad dressing**
2½ Tbsp. cornstarch	**½ cup catsup**
2½ Tbsp. sugar	**¾ tsp. salt**

1. Mix all ingredients together and bring to a boil until it thickens.
2. Pour over cooked macaroni.

Variations:

This sauce may also be used over string beans.
It is also good on onions which have been baked for ½ hour.

Corn with Cheese

1 qt. corn (drained)
1½ Tbsp butter
4 eggs
2 cups milk
1 cup cracker crumbs

½ cup grated cheese or a
little more
¾ tsp. salt
½ tsp. paprika
¼ tsp. pepper

Beat eggs. Add milk, corn and seasonings. Pour a layer of mixture into greased pan. Add shredded cheese. Pour in remainder of corn mixture. Sprinkle with cracker crumbs. Bake for 40 to 50 minutes.

Corn with Cheese

Makes 6 servings

2 eggs
1 cup milk
2 cups corn, drained
¾ tsp. butter
¼ tsp. salt

¼ tsp. paprika
⅛ tsp. pepper
½ cup grated cheddar cheese
½ cup crushed cracker crumbs

1. Beat eggs.
2. Add milk, corn, butter and seasonings.
3. Pour a layer of mixture into greased baking dish.
4. Top with shredded cheese.
5. Pour in remaining corn mixture.
6. Sprinkle with cracker crumbs.
7. Bake at 350° for 40–50 minutes.

Noodles with Meat and Cheese

4 lbs. noodles, cooked and drained
7 lbs. hamburger
1 box cheese, melted

Put half of the cooked noodles in the bottom of a greased casserole dish. Spread with browned hamburger. Coat with cheese. Add the remainder of the noodles. Bake until nice and brown.

Noodles with Meat and Cheese

Makes 4–5 servings

2½ cups noodles, cooked and drained

1 lb. hamburger, browned
¾ cup cheese, grated

1. Put half of cooked noodles in the bottom of a greased casserole dish.
2. Spread browned hamburger over top.
3. Sprinkle with cheese.
4. Add the remaining noodles.
5. Bake until golden brown at 350° for about 35 minutes.

Fried Rice

vegetable oil
3 lbs. rice, prepared
   and drained
small bowl of onions
1 qt. canned tomatoes

½ bowl water
1 Tbsp. celery salt
little coloring
little soup base

Fry cooked rice in vegetable oil with onions. Be careful so that it does not burn. Combine with canned tomatoes, water, celery salt, coloring and soup base. Bake in oven until done.

Fried Rice

Makes 6 servings

3 Tbsp. vegetable oil
2 cups cooked rice
1 small onion, chopped
1 cup canned tomatoes

¾ tsp. celery salt
½ cup soup stock or beef
   bouillon

1. Fry cooked rice and onions in vegetable oil, stirring frequently so mixture doesn't burn.
2. Add canned tomatoes, celery salt and beef stock.
3. Bake at 350° until hot, about 20–30 minutes.

Celery and Rice

Celery and Rice

6 cups raw rice
4 cups celery
2 onions
salt and pepper to taste
margarine

Cook rice in water and drain. Set aside. Fry onions and celery in margarine. Add salt and pepper. When nice and brown, mix all ingredients together and fry on hotplate.

Celery and Rice

1 cup rice	⅓ cup chopped onion
2 cups water	2 Tbsp. margarine
1 tsp. salt	salt and pepper to taste
⅔ cup celery	

1. Combine rice, water and salt in heavy 2-quart pan. Bring to hard boil uncovered. Lower heat and cover. Simmer 20 minutes.
2. Sauté onions and celery in margarine in frying pan.
3. Add salt and pepper. Add seasoned vegetables to rice.
4. Serve plain or covered with cheese or meat sauce.

Del Monico Potatoes

21 medium potatoes
3 cups shredded cheese
3 cups shredded onions
1½ cups sour cream
   thinned with a little milk

¼ lb. butter
parsley flakes
salt
pepper

Boil potatoes in skins. Refrigerate, then shred. Butter casseroles. Fill casseroles by alternating layers of potatoes, butter, cheese, onions, sour cream, salt and pepper. Top with parsley. Bake in oven at 350° for 45 minutes.

Del Monico Potatoes

Makes 6 servings

6 medium potatoes
2⅔ Tbsp. butter
1 cup shredded cheddar cheese
½ cup grated onions

½ cup sour cream, thinned
   with 2 Tbsp. milk
salt and pepper
parsley flakes

1. Boil potatoes in skins. Peel when cooled.
2. Refrigerate, then shred.
3. Fill a 2-quart buttered casserole by alternating layers of potatoes, butter, cheese, onions, sour cream, salt and pepper. Top with parsley flakes.
4. Bake at 350° for 45 minutes.

Potato Omelet

9 cups mashed potatoes
5 eggs
2¼ cups flour
2¼ tsp. baking powder
4½ tsp. onion powder

Mix well and drop by spoonful into hot fat. Fry at 375° until golden brown.

Potato Omelet

Makes 6 servings

4½ cups mashed potatoes
2 eggs
1⅛ cups flour

1 tsp. baking powder
2¼ tsp. onion powder

1. Mix well and drop by teaspoonsful into hot fat.
2. Fry at 375° until golden brown.

Corn Fritters

2¼ cups flour
2¼ tsp. baking powder
2¼ tsp. salt
1¼ cups milk

2¼ tsp. margarine
5 eggs
corn

Sift together dry ingredients. Mix together eggs, milk and butter. Add dry ingredients. Beat until smooth. Add corn, cooked and drained. Use as much corn as you like, the more the better. Fry at 370°. Drop by spoonsful into fat and fry until golden brown.

Corn Fritters

Makes 6 servings

1 cup flour
1 tsp. baking powder
2 eggs
½ cup milk

1 tsp. butter or margarine
**1½ cups corn, cooked and
    drained**

1. Sift together dry ingredients.
2. Mix together eggs, milk and butter.
3. Add dry ingredients to wet, stirring until smooth.
4. Add corn and mix.
5. Drop by teaspoonsful into hot fat (370°) and fry until golden brown.
6. Serve with syrup.

Potato Dumplings

1½ pails peeled potatoes   9 tsp. baking powder
12 cups flour   18 eggs
9 tsp. cream of tartar   ½ cup salt

Mix all ingredients together. Drop by spoonful onto broth. Cover and cook for 20 minutes. Do not lift lid while cooking.

Potato Dumplings

Makes 6 servings

4 medium-sized raw potatoes   2 eggs
1 cup flour   ¼ tsp. salt
1 tsp. cream of tartar   2 quarts meat broth
1 tsp. baking powder

1. Boil the potatoes and mash them.
2. Mix all dry ingredients together.
3. Stir dry ingredients into the mashed potatoes. Add the eggs.
4. Drop by teaspoonsful into boiling beef or chicken broth which contains chunks of meat and vegetables. Cover and let simmer for about 10 minutes.

SALADS

Fruit Salad

9 Tbsp. sugar
4 Tbsp. cornstarch
6 beaten eggs
1 tsp. salt
3 cups juice from fruit

2 cups whipped cream
1 gallon fruit cocktail
2 bags miniature marsh-
   mallows
nuts for topping

Mix together sugar, cornstarch, eggs and salt. Add juice and cook until it thickens. Cool. Add whipped cream, marshmallows and fruit. Top with nuts.

Fruit Salad

Makes 6 servings

2¼ Tbsp. sugar
1 Tbsp. cornstarch
2 beaten eggs
¼ tsp. salt
¾ cup juice from fruit
½ cup whipped cream

1 qt. fruit cocktail, drained
   (save juice)
½ bag miniature
   marshmallows
nuts for topping

1. Mix together sugar, cornstarch, eggs and salt.
2. Add juice and cook until thickened.
3. Cool. Add whipped cream, marshmallows and fruit.
4. Top with nuts.

Cold Chow

1 qt. cabbage, shredded fine
1 cup sour cream
4 Tbsp. sugar
2 tsp. salt
½ tsp. pepper
4 Tbsp. cider vinegar
½ cup green pepper pieces

Mix all ingredients together. Chill.

Cold Chow

Makes 6 servings

**2 cups finely shredded
cabbage**
½ cup sour cream
2 Tbsp. sugar

½ tsp. salt
¼ tsp. pepper
2 Tbsp. cider vinegar
¼ cup green pepper, chopped

Mix all ingredients together. Chill and serve.

Three Cucumber Salads

1. 2 qts. cucumbers, cut fine
   3 cups macaroni, cooked and drained
   ½ cup onion, cut fine

   Mix together and add salad dressing.

2. 12 eggs, cut up after hard boiling
   1½ qts. cucumbers, cut fine
   1½ cups macaroni, cooked and drained

   Mix together and add salad dressing.

3. 12 eggs, cut up after hard boiling
   2 qts. cucumbers
   1 cup dressing
   ½ onion

   Mix together and add salad dressing.

Three Cucumber Salads

Each makes 6 servings

I. 2 cups cucumber, cut fine
   3 cups macaroni, cooked
      and drained
   2 Tbsp. onion, cut fine

Mix together and add salad dressing. Serve.

II. 3 eggs, hard-boiled
       and cut up
    1¼ cups cucumber,
       cut fine
    1¼ cups macaroni, cooked
       and drained

Mix together and add salad dressing. Serve.

III. 3 eggs, hard-boiled
        and cut up
     2 cups cucumber, cut fine
     1¼ cups salad dressing
     2 Tbsp. onion,
        chopped fine

Mix together and serve.

Potato Salad

3 cups small pieces of potatoes
1 medium chopped onion
8 eggs, chopped, hard boiled
½ cup chopped green peppers
2 Tbsp. vinegar
2 cups Miracle salad dressing

Boil potatoes and drain. Cut into small pieces. Chop medium onion and add to potatoes. Boil eggs and chop. Add eggs, green peppers, vinegar and salad dressing. Mix well. Chill.

Potato Salad

Serves 6

3–4 medium-sized potatoes
½ medium onion, chopped
2 hard-boiled eggs, chopped
2 Tbsp. green pepper, finely chopped
½ Tbsp. vinegar
½ cup Miracle Whip salad dressing

1. Boil potatoes and drain. Cool. Cut into small pieces.
2. Add onion, eggs, green pepper, vinegar and salad dressing. Mix well. Chill.

Kidney Bean Salad

1 can kidney beans,
   not drained
2 big cucumbers
2 onions
1 head celery
2 green peppers

4 tomatoes
Miracle Whip salad dressing
   or mayonnaise with a
   little milk to thin
salt and pepper

Chop cucumbers, onions, celery, peppers and tomatoes.
Add kidney beans, dressing, salt and pepper. Chill.

Macaroni Salad

2 cups macaroni,
   cooked and drained
2 cups shredded cheese
2 cups sausage pieces
8 eggs, cooked and
   chopped

1 cup chopped cucumbers
1 cup chopped celery
2 cups white dressing
(salad dressing)

Combine all ingredients. Chill.

Sour Cream Sauce

2 cups milk
3 Tbsp. flour
2 Tbsp. margarine
1/2 tsp. salt
2 cups salad dressing

Combine all ingredients.

Celery and Kidney Bean Salad

1 can kidney beans,
   not drained
2 qts. celery
2 green peppers
2 jars pimentos

1 onion
Miracle Whip salad dressing
   or mayonnaise with a
   little milk to thin
salt and pepper

Chop celery, peppers, pimentos and onion. Add kidney beans, salad dressing, salt and pepper. Chill.

Celery and Kidney Bean Salad

Makes 6 servings

½ can kidney beans, not
   drained
2 cups chopped celery
1 cup chopped green peppers
1 small jar pimentos, diced

½ onion, diced
½ cup Miracle Whip or
   mayonnaise
dash of salt
dash of pepper

1. Gently stir together all vegetables.
2. Add salad dressing, salt and pepper. Chill and serve.

Pea Salad

1 lb. macaroni shells, cooked and drained
1 qt. peas, cooked
2 Tbsp. chopped onion
2 Tbsp. grated cheese
1 cup salad dressing

Combine all ingredients. Chill

Pea Salad

Makes 6 servings

2 cups cooked macaroni shells
2 cups peas, cooked
1 Tbsp. chopped onion

2 Tbsp. grated cheese
½ cup salad dressing

Combine all ingredients. Chill and serve.

Parm-a-Salad

2 cups elbow macaroni, cooked and drained
1½ cups chopped tomatoes or pimentos
1¼ cups celery pieces
¾ cup grated parmesan cheese

⅔ cup chopped dill pickles
⅔ cup chopped onions
1½ tsp. mustard
¼ tsp. pepper
1¼ cups mayonnaise

Combine all ingredients, except mayonnaise. Toss lightly. Add mayonnaise. Mix well, chill.

SOUPS
and
ODDS & ENDS

Eggplant

7 medium eggplants
1¾ cups butter
3½ cups bread crumbs
7 Tbsp. chopped onions
14 eggs, well beaten

Prepare eggplant and cut into ¼ inch slices. Cook in salted water until tender. Drain and mash. Add butter, crumbs, onion and eggs. Season to taste. Mix thoroughly. Pour into well-greased baking dish. Bake at 400° until nicely browned.

Eggplant

Makes 2–3 servings

1 medium eggplant
¼ cup butter, softened
½ cup bread crumbs

1 Tbsp. chopped onion
2 eggs, well beaten

1. Peel eggplant and cut into ¼-inch slices.
2. Boil in salted water until tender.
3. Drain and mash.
4. Add butter, crumbs, onions and eggs.
5. Season to taste. Mix thoroughly.
6. Pour into well-greased baking dish.
7. Bake at 400° until nicely browned.

Tomato Soup

2 gallons tomato juice   ½ cup brown sugar
¼ lb. margarine   1 Tbsp. onion salt
1 cup flour dissolved   ½ tsp. pepper
   in 2 cups water   1½ Tbsp. baking soda dissolved
1 Tbsp. celery seed   in ½ dipper of milk

Combine all ingredients in sauce pan and heat.

Tomato Soup

Makes 3 servings

2 cups tomato juice
1 Tbsp. margarine
⅛ cup flour dissolved in
¼ cup water
⅓ tsp. celery seed

3 Tbsp. brown sugar
⅓ tsp. onion salt
⅛ tsp. pepper
1 tsp. baking soda dissolved in
1 cup milk

Combine all ingredients in sauce pan and heat.

Split Pea Soup

1 bag peas with enough water to cover
2 onions
2 Tbsp. salt
1 tsp. pepper
½ gallon cream or milk

Cook peas, water, onions, salt and pepper by boiling for about 2 hours. Add cream or milk.

Split Pea Soup

Makes 4 servings

½ small bag of split peas,
   covered with
     3 cups cold water
½ onion, chopped

½ tsp. salt
¼ tsp. pepper
2 cups milk

1. Soak dry peas in water overnight.
2. Simmer peas, water, onions, salt and pepper together for 1 hour.
3. Add milk and heat.

Chili Soup

4 cups raw kidney beans
enough water to cover
   after cooking beans
10 cups tomatoes,
   cooked and beaten

1½ jars tomato juice
5½ lbs. ground beef
3½ cups chopped onions
¼ cup chili powder

Cook kidney beans in water. When done, add enough water to cover. Add ten cups tomatoes, cooked and beaten, and 1½ jars tomato juice. Set aside. Fry together beef, onions and chili powder. Combine two mixtures and simmer until flavors are well blended, about 10 minutes.

Chili Soup

Makes 5 servings

1 cup raw red kidney beans
   with 1 tsp. salt
water to cover cooked beans
2 cups tomatoes, cooked and
   mashed

1 lb. ground beef
¾ cup chopped onion
2 tsp. chili powder
salt and pepper to taste

1. Cook kidney beans in salted water.
2. When done add additional water if needed to cover.
3. Add tomatoes and tomato juice. Set this mixture aside.
4. Fry together beef, onions, chili powder, salt and pepper. Combine two mixtures and simmer about 10 minutes.

Mixed Cream of Potato Soup

2 qts. potatoes   ½ gallon cream
4 onions   1 Tbsp. chicken base
3 qts. water   1 Tbsp. beef base

Cook potatoes and onions until real tender. Blend. Add cream and soup bases.

Mixed Cream of Potato Soup

Makes 4–5 servings

2 cups potatoes	1 tsp. chicken base
1 onion	1 tsp. beef base
3 cups water	
2 cups cream or 1 can evaporated milk plus regular milk to make 2 cups	

1. Peel and dice potatoes and onion. Cook in water until quite tender.
2. Add the milk and soup base to the potatoes and heat over low burner, but do not boil.

Bean Soup

1 dipper beans
1½ dippers water
3 onions
2 Tbsp. beef soup base
½ gallon milk or cream

Cook beans, water and onions until tender. add soup base and milk or cream.

Bean Soup

Makes 4 servings

½ lb. dry navy beans	**1 Tbsp. beef soup base or**
4 cups hot water	**2 beef bouillon cubes**
1 onion, chopped	**4 cups milk**

1. Rinse beans. Soak beans in hot water for 2 hours.
2. Boil beans in same water until partly done.
3. Add onions and bouillon. Bring to boil and continue cooking until beans are soft.
4. Add milk and reheat.

Special Menus
Sunset Colony, Schmiedeleut

WEDDING
Beef and noodle soup
Boiled potatoes
Head lettuce with fresh vegetables (purchased, if necessary)
Red jello with fruit cocktail
Homemade buns (commercial bread purchased, in case of need)
Various relishes, pickles, jellies and sauces
White cupcakes early in day
Dark cupcakes later in day
Four-layer wedding cake of four different colors
Special cake for preachers in shape of a book

FUNERAL
Beef and noodle soup (noodles may be replaced with buckwheat and eggs)
Boiled potatoes
Sauerkraut with sugar
Fresh lettuce and vegetable salad (purchased, if necessary)
Red jello with fruit cocktail
Various relishes, pickles, jellies and sauces
Commercial bread (too many people to serve homemade bread)

THANKSGIVING
Duck, boiled and roasted
Noodle soup in poultry base
Boiled potatoes
Cooked sauerkraut
Coleslaw
Pickles
Homemade buns
Cranberry sauce
Pumpkin pie

Mixed Cream of Vegetable Soup

2 cups carrots
2 cups beans
2 cups peas
2 cups celery or use
a little celery seed

3 Tbsp. onion salt
½ gallon cream
2 Tbsp. soup base

Cook carrots, beans, peas, celery and onion salt until tender. Blend. Add cream and soup base.

Mixed Cream of Vegetable Soup

Makes 4 servings

½ cup carrots
½ cup beans
½ cup peas
½ cup celery or 1 tsp. celery
  seed
1 tsp. onion salt

2 cups cream or 1 can
  evaporated milk plus
  regular milk to make 2 cups
1½ tsp. soup base
salt and pepper to taste

1. Simmer carrots, beans, peas, celery and onion salt until vegetables are tender.
2. Add cream, soup base and seasonings. Heat and serve.

Celery and Macaroni Soup

3 cups macaroni, cooked a little raw and drained
2 dippers water
1 qt. celery pieces
2 cups onion pieces
1 Tbsp. beef soup base

Cook macaroni until nearly done and drain. In 2 dippers water, cook celery and onion. When done, add to macaroni, along with beef base. Do not cook anymore.

Celery and Macaroni Soup

Makes 5 servings

1 cup dry macaroni
1⅓ cups chopped celery
⅔ cup chopped onion
4 cups water

1 Tbsp. beef soup base or
  2 beef bouillon cubes
salt and pepper to taste

1. Cook macaroni until nearly done. Drain.
2. Cook onions and celery in water.
3. Add beef base or bouillon and the macaroni.
4. Warm again but do not boil.

Ground Carrot Soup

2 dippers of water   3 cups milk
½ qt. ground carrots   2 Tbsp. chicken soup base
¾ lb. cheese

Cook carrots in 2 dippers water for about 1 hour. Add cheese which has been melted in milk. add more milk if you desire and chicken soup base.

Ground Carrot Soup

Makes 4 servings

2 cups water	**2 cups milk**
⅔ cup ground raw carrots	**2 Tbsp. flour**
¼ lb. cheddar cheese, grated	**1 tsp. chicken base**

1. Cook carrots in water for about 1 hour.
2. Thicken the milk with the flour.
3. Add the shredded cheese to the milk.
4. Add the boiled carrots, water and chicken base to the milk.
5. Heat and serve.

Onion Ring Batter

3 cups flour
3 tsp. baking powder
1 tsp. salt

3 eggs, well beaten
3 cups milk
⅛ cup salad oil

Cut onion rings a little thin, but not too thin. Then flour them and dip them into the above batter. Fry at 200° until golden brown.

Onion Ring Batter

Makes 6 servings

1½ cups flour
1½ tsp. baking powder
¼ tsp. salt
2 eggs, well beaten

1¼ cups milk
1 Tbsp. salad oil
onions for dipping

1. Cut onion rings thin but not too thin (about ⅓ inch thick).
2. Mix all ingredients together (except onions) until smooth. Dip onion rings in batter.
3. Fry at 200° until golden brown.

Batter for Frying Chicken Chunks

1 qt. milk
1 qt. eggs
2 Tbsp. salt
½ tsp. pepper
bread crumbs

Mix eggs, milk, salt and pepper. Dip chicken pieces in flour, then the above batter, then bread crumbs. Fry at 300° until golden brown.

Batter for Frying Chicken Chunks

1 cup eggs
1 cup milk
½ tsp. salt

¼ tsp. pepper
bread crumbs

1. Mix eggs, milk, salt and pepper.
2. Dip chicken pieces in flour, then in the above mixture, then in fine bread crumbs.
3. Fry at 300° until golden brown.

French Fried Onion Rings

onion rings
milk
flour
finely crushed crackers

Fry onion rings a few at a time at 365° until golden brown after dipping in milk, flour, milk and cracker crumbs.

CANNING

Ready to Eat Refrigerator Pickles

4 gallons sliced cucumbers
1 qt. green peppers, sliced
1 qt. onions, sliced
½ cup salt
½ cup celery seed

Brine

2 qts. water
2 qts. vinegar
1 gallon sugar

Sprinkle salt and celery seed over all and mix well. Mix cold water, vinegar and sugar. Stir well and pour over cold cucumber mixture.

Seal cold and store in refrigerator. Keeps well for months.

Ice Pickles

10 (3 gallon size) stainless steel pails of thinly sliced cucumbers
40 medium onions
¾ cup dried red pepper
45 garlic pieces

Brine

3 gallons vinegar
½ cup turmeric
¼ cup celery seed
5 gallons sugar

Mix onions and cucumbers and soak for 3 hours in salted water in freezer. (1 cup salt to 1 stainless pail water) Drain water from cucumbers. Pour sugar, spices and vinegar over cucumbers and bring to a full boil.

Fill jars and seal at once.

Hamburger Pickles (also Peppers)

2 qts. cucumbers
1 qt. onions
1 qt. sugar
½ cup salt

1 qt. vinegar
1 tsp. turmeric
1 tsp. celery seed
1 tsp. mustard seed

Pack cucumbers and onions in ½ gallon jars. Pour brine over filled jars. Store in cooler. Can also use pails.

Hot Peppers

lg.	med.	sm.	
5	2½	1¼	gallons water
5	2½	1¼	gallons vinegar
3	1½	¾	cups alum
20	10	5	cups sugar
4½	2¼	1⅛	cups salt
1	½	¼	cup turmeric

Boil brine 5 minutes, then pour over peppers. Blanch peppers before putting in pails just to get more in the pails.

Hamburger Pickles

2½ gallons water
1¼ gallons vinegar
1½ cups pickling salt

2 Tbsp. alum
2 Tbsp. turmeric

Mix all ingredients together and boil for 5 minutes. Pack jars with sliced corrugated cucumbers. Add dill and garlic to each jar. Fill with hot brine and seal immediately.
This recipe should make 40 qt. jars.

Peeled Cucumber Pickles

10 gallons cucumbers,
  peeled and sliced
2½ cups salt

20 medium onions
10 cups vinegar
20 cups sugar

Prepare first 3 ingredients and let stand for 24 hours. Drain the next day, then add sugar and vinegar, and let stand for 24 hours. Then they are ready to serve or freeze.

Thick Dill Pickles

1 gallon vinegar
1 gallon sugar
3 gallons water

Mix this and bring to a boil. Cut cucumbers in thick slices. Fill jars. Add 3 garlic pieces, a little dill and 1 Tbsp. salt to each jar.

Place in hot water for at least 15 minutes, close to a boiling point. Do not boil. Just keep in water until pickles change color.

Pickled Watermelons

8 3-gallon pails water
4½ gallons sugar
4½ gallons vinegar

Boil brine for 5 minutes.
Fill jars with cut-up watermelon. In each jar put ¼ of pimento, 2 pieces of garlic and a little dill.
Don't put salt in brine. Put 1 Tbsp. in each jar.

Sweet Pickle Sticks

Cut cucumbers into sticks lengthwise. Pour boiling water over them and let stand 4 to 5 hours.
Drain and pack into jars.

Brine

3 qts. and 1 cup vinegar
3 qts. sugar
3/4 cup salt

6 Tbsp. celery seed
6 Tbsp. turmeric
1 Tbsp. mustard seed

Boil this solution for 5 minutes. Fill jars and steam for 5 minutes. This brine doubled is for 15 1/2 gallon jars.

Small Sweet Pickles

Soak very small whole cucumbers in salt water overnight. In the morning drain salt water from cukes.

Brine

1 gallon water
2 3/4 qts. vinegar
2 qts. sugar

3 Tbsp. salt
3 Tbsp. allspice

Bring this brine to a boil and add cucumbers only till they change color. Do not boil.
Fill in hot jars to seal.

Open Jar Pickles

12 gallons	1 gallon cucumbers, small, cut in half lengthwise
6 cups	Pour ½ cup pickling salt and
6 Tbsp.	1½ tsp. alum over clean cut-up cucumbers. Cover with boiling water and let stand overnight. In the morning drain and wipe dry, then put in crock or container.
	Add the following:
6 gallons	½ gallon vinegar (should cover pickles; if not add a little more)
3 cups	4 Tbsp. sugar
3 cups	4 Tbsp. pickling spice
¾ cup	1 Tbsp. celery seed
¾ cup	1 Tbsp. mustard seed
18 quarts	Add ½ cup sugar each morning until 6 cups are added. Mix well into pickles each time.

For the big recipe add (sugar) 6 cups each day, till 18 qts. are used.

Pickled Peppers

3 gallons water   3 cups pickling salt
1 gallon vinegar   1 cup sugar

Put peppers in ½-gallon jars. Add a little dill and 2 small pieces of garlic.

Mix water, vinegar, salt and sugar. Bring to a boil. Bring to a boil.

Pour on jars of filled peppers. Seal and steam for 30 minutes.

Steam like pickled cucumbers; water should not boil too hard.

Vegetable - Cauliflower Mixed Pickled

Fill ½-gallon jars with cauliflower, carrot strips, small onions, few cucumbers, chunks of celery and pepper strips.

Cook cauliflower and carrot strips for 15 minutes, but don't take the juice.

Mix 5 qts. water
    1½ qts. vinegar
    1 cup salt
    1 cup sugar
    1 Tbsp. alum
    a little pickling spice

Fill jars with mixed vegetables. Pour brine on jars boiling hot.

Boil brine for 15 minutes.

Enlarge this recipe 10 times for 40 ½-gallon jars. Steam for 30 minutes. Don't let it boil too hard.

It needs 3 heaping bushels of cauliflower for this recipe.

Relish

24 18 qts. ground cucumbers soaked with 1½ cups salt for 3 hours before using.

Drain and mix.

6   4 qts. carrots
16 12 green peppers
32 24 medium onions
8   6 jars pimentos
6   4½ qts. vinegar
8   6 qts. sugar
8   6 tsp. ground mustard
16 12 tsp. turmeric

Mix together and cook for 30 minutes. Fill jars and seal at once.

Mixed Sweet and Sour Vegetable Pickles

4 lbs pickling cucumbers, cut up
1 or 2 pickling onions
2 sweet green peppers, cut up
2 sweet red peppers, cut up
1 head cauliflower
2 or 3 carrots, cut in sticks

Cover with ½ cup pickling salt. Mix with ice cubes and let sit for 3 hours. Then drain.

Combine:

4 cups sugar
½ tsp. whole spice
2 tsp. celery seed
1½ Tbsp. mustard seed
1 qt. vinegar

Bring to a boil and let boil 3 minutes. Add drained vegetables and bring to a boil. Pack in jars and steam for 5 minutes.

Next time: Try adding salt to brine, filling the jars with raw vegetables and steam longer than 5 minutes. It's too well done and messy the recipe way.
Add hot peppers when we have some.

Cucumber Relish

4 gallons green tomatoes
4 gallons cucumbers
12 sweet red peppers
12 green peppers
4 large heads celery
4 qts. onions

Grind the vegetables and sprinkle with 4 cups salt. Cover with boiling water and allow to stand 30 minutes, then drain. Cover with mild vinegar, about 2 gallons.

12 Tbsp. ground mustard
4 Tbsp. turmeric
1 gallon sugar
3 cups flour

Mix the above to a smooth paste with cold water. Add to ground vegetables. Bring to a good boiling point, then put into jars to seal.
Makes 23 ½ gallon jars.

Mustard Beans

½	3 3-gallon stainless pails cut-up string beans
½	3 3-gallon pails cut-up cucumbers
1½ qt.	2 gallon and 1 qt. brown sugar
1	6 cups flour
1	6 qts. vinegar
½	3 cups mustard powder
3 Tbsp.	¾ cup turmeric
3 Tbsp.	¾ cup celery seed

Cook string beans soft and drain. Salt cucumbers over-night. Mix flour, mustard, turmeric and celery seed. Make a paste with the vinegar. Pour sugar over beans, then mix with the rest. Bring to a boil and fill jars immediately.

Corn Relish

21 gallons	5 gallons raw sweet corn
28 medium	7 medium heads cabbage (shredded)
56 each	28 peppers (14 red and 14 green)
112 medium	28 medium onions
7 gallons	1¾ gallons sugar
5¼ gallons	1¼ gallons vinegar
5 cups	1⅓ cups salt
2 cups	½ cup mustard seed
1 cup	7 Tbsp. celery salt

Boil for 20 minutes. Fill jars and seal at once.

Blanching Beans

Bring water to a rolling boil. Put beans in sieve and place in boiling water for 4 minutes.
Take out at once and cool in ice cold water. Drain and freeze.

Canning Beans

Fill jars with beans, add 1 Tbsp. salt and water. Steam for 4 hours.

Canning Whole Beets

Wash and cook beets until skins peel off. Fill jars with beets and add 1 tsp. salt to each jar. Fill with hot water. Seal and steam for 1½ hours.
(2 bushels beets make 18- half- gallon jars)

Beet Pieces

Cook 2 bushels beets so they can be peeled. Put in cold water and cut in small pieces.

Brine

2 gallons vinegar   2 gallons sugar
4 gallons water   1 Tbsp. spice, wrapped in cloth

Bring to a boil, then dump in beets and let them boil again. Fill jars as fast as possible. Steam for 10 minutes.

1986, we had 9 black garden boxes canned
    41 half- gallon jars, whole
    20 half- gallon jars, pieces

Freezing Peaches

6 cups water
5 cups sugar
1 6 oz. can frozen orange juice

Boil and pour over fruit, enough to cover and freeze.

Canning Peas

Fill jars with peas, then add 1 tsp. salt, 1 tsp. sugar and 1 tsp. vinegar to each jar. Seal jars and steam for 3½ hours.

Canning Carrots

Wash carrots and remove tips. Cut into pieces. Put into clean hot jars. Add 1 Tbsp. salt and fill with water. Seal and steam for 2½ hours.

Canning Broccoli

Break flowerettes and wash thoroughly. Fill jars with broccoli. Add 1 tsp. salt and fill with water. Steam for 1 hour and 30 minutes.

Cream-Style Sweet Corn

2½ gallons and 2 cups water
1½ qts. sugar
¾ cup salt

Mix and bring to boil, then add 7½ gallons corn. Cook for 5 minutes; let cool. Fill containers and freeze the next day. Cut corn from cob when raw.

7 gallons from 1 batch (1 recipe)
20 batches equals 136 gallons.

Applesauce

Cook apples soft. Put through juicer, then mix:

5 pails applesauce
1 pail sugar

Fill jars and steam for 35 minutes.

Canning Chicken

Prepare cut-up chicken by soaking with 1 cup salt to 3 gallons water for 10 minutes.

Fill clean jars and add 1 Tbsp. salt to each ½-gallon jar.

Steam for 5 hours.

It needs 1¾ chicken to each ½ gallon jar. For 145 jars, cut 243 chickens. (About 180 chickens for 114 jars.)

Canning Fish

1 pail water
1 cup salt
fish
½ cup vinegar
1 Tbsp. salt

Soak fish in water and salt for 15 to 20 minutes. Drain well. Put ½ cup vinegar in the bottom of ½ gallon jar, along with 1 Tbsp. salt. Pack fish in jars as tightly as possible. Steam for 6½ hours.

Chokecherries Gooseberry Jam

4 cups chokeberries
2 cups gooseberries
water
sugar
1 bottle Certo

Put fruit in saucepan and add enough water to cover. Boil for 10 minutes on medium heat. Remove from heat and put through sieve to obtain juice. Measure the juice and add the same amount of sugar.
Boil hard for ten minutes and add Certo. Boil for one more minute. Pour into jars and seal. Turn upside down to seal.

Chokecherry Jelly

Wash cherries thoroughly, then add enough water to cover the cherries, or even a little less, because if the liquid is too water-like, its very hard to get a jelly consistency and you have to boil it longer. We cooked it for 5 minutes and had to re-cook it for another 5 minutes at least. Otherwise cook as directed on Sure-Jell label.

Strawberry Jam

5 cups strawberries
5 cups sugar
1 box Sure-Jell

Cook as directed on Sure-Jell label. After sugar is added cook for 1 minute (hard).
We cooked jam on Sept. 30 in brazing pan - 24 of the above batches at a time.

Apple Juice

4 pails big cut-up apples
5 pails crab apples
8 pails water

Put apples and water in cooker and let them in there till the apples are cracked up nicely.

Scoop everything out in a large container and let stand for ½ to one hour, so the taste comes out in juice more.

Drain juice from apples and sieve 3 to 4 times through cheesecloth or more closely woven cloth.

Put ⅓ cup sugar in each ½ gallon jar. Steam for 20 minutes.

Tomato Juice

8 stainless steel 3-gallon pails tomatoes
2 qts. carrots
1 qt. onions

1 heaping qt. beets
1 qt. celery
1 qt. green pepper
1 qt. parsley

Cook the vegetables separately. When soft add to tomatoes. Add 1 cup salt and 1 qt. sugar to a large stainless steel container of tomato juice. Fill jars and steam for ½ hour.

Tomato Ketchup

10 gallons	5 gallons tomato juice
16 lbs	8 lbs. sugar
40 medium	20 medium onions
1 gallon + 1 qt.	½ gallon and two cups vinegar
1 cup	⅔ cup allspice
2¾ cups	1½ cups celery seed
2¾ cups	1½ cups salt
1 cup	½ cup ground cloves

First grind tomatoes. Cook till soft, then put in or on sack to drain water for a couple of hours. Put through juicer, then add all ingredients and cook for ½ hour. (Put cloves, allspice and celery seed in cheesecloth.) Fill jars and seal. Do not steam.

Syrups for Canning

Heavy — 2 parts sugar and 2 parts water
Medium — 2 parts water and 1 part sugar
Thin — 3 parts water and 1 part sugar

Fruits	Cooking Time in Jars	Syrup
Peaches	30 minutes	medium
Apricots	30 minutes	medium
Cherries	30 minutes	thin
Pears	30 minutes	medium
Plums	35 minutes	medium
Apples	35 minutes	medium
Tomatoes	45 minutes	medium
Grapes	30 minutes	thin

1978 Canning Year

June 13	Rhubarb for Pie	12 bags
	Rhubarb for Sat.	13 bags
June 15	Chicken	
	(cut up 130 chickens)	63 jars
June 29	Broccoli	41 jars
July 19	Whole Beets	36 qts.
	Beet Pieces	58 qts.
July 19	Peas	107 jars
July 26	Peas	53 jars
	Peas froze	21 bags
July 20	Stringbeans	470 jars
		80 jars
		113 jars
		663 jars
Aug. 24	Vegetable Soup	21 jars
July 24	Cherries	110 jars
	Cherries froze	31 cans
	Cherries for Jam froze	12 cans
July 24	Nectarines	53 jars

1986 Canning Year

April 21	Celery	unblanched froze	40 bags
May 15	Rhubarb		16 bags
May 15	Spinach	unblanched	12 bags
May 29	Chicken	(175)	114 jars
June 13	Strawberries		2 cans
June 16	Strawberries		4 cans
June 18	Strawberries		3 cans
June 20	Strawberries		8 cans
June 22	Strawberries		7 cans
June 25	Strawberries		5 cans
June 27	Strawberries		2 cans
July 1	Strawberries		1 can
June 16	Gooseberries		6 bags
July 1	Whole Beets		41 jars
July 1	Beet Pieces		20 jars
July 9	Peas		51 jars
July 16	Peas		35 jars
			86 jars
July 9	Chard	unblanched	10 bags
July 12	Cauliflower	froze	21 pails
July 15	Cauliflower	pickled	38 jars
July 12	Cherries		62 jars
July 17	Cherries		150 jars
			212 jars

July 17	Peaches	55 jars
Aug 4	Peaches	214 jars
		269 jars
Aug 4	Peaches froze	8 cans
July 14	Ice Pickles	45 jars
July 21	Hamburger Pickles	30 qts.
July 21	Sweet Dill Pickles	30 jars
July 23	Sweet Pickle Sticks	15 jars
July 22	Open Jar Pickles	10 gallons
July 26	Small Sweet Cukes	30 jars
July 29	Cucumber Relish	14 jars
July 29	String beans	237 jars
Aug 5	String beans	110 jars
July 22	String beans	159 jars
		506 jars
Aug. 1	Carrots	116 jars
Aug. 6	Chokecherry Jelly	21 jars
Aug. 7	Froze Corn	136 gallons
Aug. 14	Apple Juice	114 jars
Aug. 15	Apple Juice	218 jars
		332 jars
Aug. 15	Small apples	25 jars
Aug. 15	Applesauce	117 jars
Sept. 26	apples	114 jars
Sept. 29	Pears	250 jars

Sept. 30	Strawberry Jam	42 pails
Sept. 11	Ketchup	27 jars
Aug. 21	Tomato Juice	92 jars
Aug. 28	Tomato Juice	200 jars
Sept. 1	Tomato Juice	148 jars
Sept. 4	Tomato Juice	346 jars
Sept. 11	Tomato Juice	174 jars
		960 jars
Sept. 1	Tomatoes	115 jars
Aug. 1	Hamburger Pickles	87 qt. jars
Aug. 10	Hamburger Pickles	11½ jars
Aug. 25	Hamburger Pickles	29 jars
Sept. 1	Hamburger Pickles	67 jars
		150 jars
Aug. 10	Ice Pickles	40 jars
Sept. 1	Ice Pickles	43 jars
		83 jars
Aug. 11	Cucumber Dills	16 jars
Aug. 18	Cucumber Dills	10 jars
Aug. 21	Cucumber Dills	22 jars
Aug 25	Cucumber Dills	32 jars
Sept. 1	Cucumber Dills	97 jars
		178 jars
Aug. 11	Froze Corn	10 gallons
Aug. 15	Froze Corn	47 gallons
Aug. 18	Froze Corn	11 gallons
Sept. 6	Froze Corn	22 gallons
		90 gallons
Sept. 9	Carrots	112 jars

Index

Readings and Sources

Bennett, John W. *Hutterian Brethren.* Stamford, California: Stamford University Press, 1967.

Gross, Paul S. *The Hutterite Way.* Saskatoon, Saskatchewan: Freeman Publishing Company, 1965.

Hofer, John. *The History of the Hutterites.* Elie, Manitoba: Educational Committee, Jones Valley Colony, 1988.

Hostetler, John A. *Hutterite Life.* Scottdale, Pennsylvania: Herald Press, 1983.

Hostetler, John A. *Hutterite Society.* Baltimore: Johns Hopkins University Press, 1974.

Hostetler, John A. and Huntington, Gertrude Enders. *The Hutterites in North America.* New York: Holt, Rinehart and Winston, 1987.

Hutterian Brethren. *The Chronicle of the Hutterian Brethren, Volume I.* Rifton, New York: Plough Publishing House, 1987.

Peter, Karl A. *The Dynamics of Hutterite Society: An Analytical Approach.* Edmonton, Alberta: The University of Alberta Press, 1987.

Peters, Victor. *All Things Common: The Hutterian Way of Life.* Minneapolis: University of Minnesota Press, 1965.

About the Author

Joanita M. Kant is Executive Director of the Codington County Historical Society and its museums in Watertown, South Dakota. She is the co-editor of *The Civil War Diary of Arthur Calvin Melette* and editor of *A History of South Dakota Century Farms.*

A graduate of the University of South Dakota, Kant lives in Watertown with her husband and daughter and serves as chairperson of the local historical preservation commission.